John Gill

MASTER OF ROCK

For Jeff
friend of this
terrain –
Pat Ament
Aug 14, 1998

John Gill

MASTER OF ROCK

REVISED AND EXPANDED

Pat Ament
with writings by John Gill

STACKPOLE
BOOKS

Published by
STACKPOLE BOOKS
5067 Ritter Road
Mechanicsburg, PA 17055

Printed in the United States

10 9 8 7 6 5 4 3 2 1

Front cover photograph: John Gill, Pueblo, Colorado
Cover design by Wendy Reynolds

In cooperation with Two Lights
10550 Quail Street
Westminster, CO 80021

Cataloging-in-Publication information is on file with Library of Congress.

I dedicate this book affectionately to Tim and Kim Shultz
Who give me hope because of their faith and love

And

To the memory of Bernice Alman Gill, John's mother,
Who passed away February 2, 1998, at the age of eighty-eight

Contents

Preface, ix
A Note About The Author, by John Gill, xii
The Solitude Of Mastery, 1
Gill's Parents, 3
Boy With Dogs and Alligators For Friends, 3
Buildering And Loft Climbing—Gill's First Ascents, 4
Catching Sharks, 5
"Unathletic Son" Excels At Climbing, 8
Rambling Wreck, 16
Forty Foot Slide To The Bottom, 19
First Visit To The Blackhills, Tetons, and Estes Park, 20
Speed Rope Climbing And Gymnastics, 21
Chalk, Its First Use In Climbing, 21
Cowboy Country, 26
America's First 5.10 Routes, 27
One-Finger Pull-Up, 33
Chalk At Devil's Lake, 33
The *Center Route* On Red Cross Rock, 38
Weather Forecaster, 39
Nearly Lost In The Hourglass, 41
Frisbee Throwing With Garbage-Can Lids, 42
The Daunting Thimble Route—The First 5.12, 44
Hagermeister Boulders, 54
Not Just A Show Of Strength, 64
Impressions From The Needles, 65
Marriage, 65
Alabama, 66
Rearick's Challenge, 69
Climbing In The South, 79
"I Recall My RDs Slipping A Bit," 93
The Move To Colorado, 96
Trips To Veedauwoo, 113
One-Arm Front Lever And The Art Of Bouldering, 117

Attempting A Gill Route, 122
Gill As Friend And Inspiration, 123
Injury And "Down-Time," 126
Telekinesis And Levitation, 128
Pueblo, 130
A New Marriage, 134
"Can You Hold It Right There?," 138
"Get The Hell Off That Rock," 140
Fireside Chat, 141
Advice On Training, 146
Master Of Rock, 148
Lost Canyon, 148
Polar Bears And Quiet Towers, 149
New Blood, 150
He Didn't Care, 162
Mystical States, 163
Tachycardia, 165
Pueblo West And A Trip To England, 165
"Failure" On Red Cross Rock, 167
Right Biceps Muscle Tears Loose From Elbow, 169
Return To *Delicate Arete,* 171
Life Savers, 172
The Experience Is Everything, 180
Dorothy, 184
Award For Excellence, 186
Grampa Gumby, 188
Repeats Of The Thimble, 191
Ribs, 195
Climbers Of A New Age Honor Gill, 197
Spiritual Apotheosis, A Reflection, 202
Duffers, 207
Index, 211

Preface

This is a lot better book than the previous two editions. Let me share a little of the history of the three different books.

When I wrote the first *Master of Rock* in 1976, I was fortunate to have it published by a real professional—Bob Godfrey. My only criticism was that he added the subtitle *the Biography of John Gill.* I had intended only a short, personal perspective of the rock climbing of Gill. The book became almost instantly out of print and a prize for collectors, often selling at used bookstores for a hundred dollars.

When Godfrey came down with Parkinson's Disease some years later and committed suicide, his remaining copies of *Master of Rock* fell prey to several climbing friends of his who seemed to rush his house and proclaim themselves his heirs. Out of courtesy, I was eventually phoned and told to come and claim a few copies that were left after the vultures had departed. I was informed by one person not to ask where the bulk of Godfrey's copies of *Master of Rock* had gone. I soon would notice copies for sale in used bookstores, sold either out of greed or unwittingly for a pittance of what they were worth. At Bob's house, I was told I also would be welcome to any other books I desired. My eyes went to a small collection of poems by Robert Creeley. In astonishment, I immediately opened the book to a sentence Godfrey had underlined: "Men kill themselves because they are afraid of death."

For years, people asked me why I would not reprint the book. My answer was that I was not satisfied with the writing. I was a relative beginner at the time of the writing and also, according to a few critics, had injected more of myself into the story than was needed. Others disagreed with such criticism and told me they especially liked my personal stories. Whichever was ultimately true, I imagined that I would do another, better book when the time came that the Spirit moved me.

At last, in 1990, I was given an opportunity to republish the book. For the second edition, I hoped to make something closer to a true biography—yet one that did not leave out the best parts of the first book. Unfortunately I was working nights and on-call as a counselor to kids at the Boulder Juvenile Center and was sorely lacking in sleep. I had to struggle and even short cut some of the tasks to put the new *Master of Rock* together. Trying to wrap up the book late one night, I made a few errors in the photo captions and even left off a couple. So it would still not be the perfect book. Yet improvements were made in the second edition, as Gill provided some wonderful writing and old photos of his youth. The end result of the second edition was a "monograph," as Jon Krakauer correctly identified it. There were no chapter titles. The edition had a dark, slightly dismal feel—something along the lines of how I felt those days.

Now with Stackpole Books publishing the book, and finding myself in a position to work on the book in the right environment and spirit and do it right, once and for all, I have created what I feel is the best *Master of Rock*.

I have revised the book, fixed errors, captioned photos that before were left off or incorrect, and I have added small sections of fascinating new information, new bits of history or material revealing Gill's recent activities. I had a great day in Pueblo with Gill, in October 1997, photographing him with a telephoto lens as he free soloed a granite tower about three hundred and fifty feet high.

In this sacred task of trying to make a study of John Gill's life, and attempting to share the remarkable vision that he defines, I have—in all editions—hoped to please a number of audiences. I trust this book may inspire individuals who simply enjoy literature and who may be interested in an unusual individual's remarkable life. I also hope to provide a book for boulderers who like to study photos and use them as a kind of "guide" (or perhaps historical guide) to different locations. While intending this book to be a kind of journal, capturing the appreciation so many climbers feel for John Gill, I hope it will prove also to be a "personal scrapbook" for John—a book that, in some worthy way, expresses his life.

I have tried to make as the soul of the book the lighthearted spirit of Gill, his hilarious stories and wonderful, small points of humor. Really it is the biography of a very good-natured man, who incidentally is also a genius and remarkable rock climber.

I am grateful to John for sharing with me the events of his life and for his assistance with the writing of the book—often sending me little stories, as they came to his mind. I am grateful to Dorothy Gill for her photos and textual insights. I must express thanks to those who have contributed to any or all three of the editions: Chris Jones, Jim Holloway, Curt Shannon, Lew Hoffman, Warren Banks, Bob Williams, Pete DeLannoy, Paul Muehl, Scott Blunk, John Sherman, and also all the original contributors to the first edition, Dave Rearick, Paul Mayrose, Steve Wunsch, Paul Piana, Bob Candelaria, Bob Kamps, Tom Higgins, David Breashears, Yvon Chouinard, Jim Erickson, and Bob Godfrey. I owe a lot to Ed Serr for his help with the layout and word processing of the second edition of the book. He kept the basic text on file, fortunately, and saved a lot of work when the time rolled around, somewhat unexpectedly, for yet another edition.

We have been forced to leave some of the photos in this book uncredited, since many were offhand snapshots by people or friends from the past whose names would require, at best, a guess. Lora Sara Frisch, however, undoubtedly took a large number of the book's older photos, during the 1960's, and Rich Borgman took a few of the photos from Fort Collins. Let this serve as grateful acknowledgement to them.

—Pat Ament, May 28, 1998

A Note About The Author, By John Gill

I met Pat Ament in 1967. Our meeting was, I think, inevitable, for there were similarities in our approaches to climbing. We both were gymnasts, although I had by then drifted away from my specialties—the still rings and rope. Pat could do a straight-body press to a handstand on the floor, followed by a number of handstand pushups, a feat that I would have been hard pressed to equal in my heyday. We both viewed climbing as essentially a gymnastic activity and both felt that bouldering was a valued and separate form of the sport. We felt that perhaps here was the best place to implement our acrobatic talents and push standards. And we also recognized other, rarely perceived dimensions of the game.

Being ten years older than Pat, I had started somewhat earlier than he, but it appears we tread the same general path independently. I began the occasional use of chalk for climbing purposes in 1954 after starting gymnastics at Georgia Tech. I first used it in midnight adventures on the old Tech campus and on Stone Mountain, then introduced it in the Tetons. Pat also discovered its usefulness in climbing a few years later in Boulder, Colorado, applying it to longer climbs as well as to bouldering.

Pat and I both learned impressive physical tricks, which included a one-finger pull-up and one-arm front lever in my case and, in Pat's case, a one-arm mantel on a narrow surface and a very controlled muscle-up on a high bar (going over slowly with both arms at the same time). I was impressed with this athletic and very accomplished young man. He had established severe bouldering routes at Flagstaff Mountain in Boulder and in Yosemite, and he had pushed up the standards of free climbing in Colorado and elsewhere considerably (beginning with his very impressive, milestone ascent of the famous *Supremacy Crack*).

Pat, who does not shy away from verbal confrontation, is unfairly attacked at times for his putative climbing styles—a very minor percentage of flaws during a formative era in American rock climbing. Those who criticize fail to consider the evolution of paradigm over time. In the 1960's, free climbing was separating from its casual involvement in mixed climbs. This was a period of experimentation, and those who boldly experimented were the movers and shakers of the era. They ultimately defined climbing for years to come.

Pat and I began visiting one another, trying each other's boulder problems. I would sometimes have difficulty with his climbs, and he would sometimes have difficulty with mine. This was to be expected, for we both realized that much climbing difficulty is relative to the size and reach of the participants. And one simply does the best one can.

In my down-time in Fort Collins—as I recovered from climber's elbow—I showed Pat several potential granite boulder problems I had discovered. He was climbing brilliantly and polished off the routes, one after the other.

Over the course of the next several years, I had the enviable opportunity to meet several of Pat's proteges who went on to become outstanding and well-known climbers: David Breashears and Christian Griffith are two who quickly come to mind.

When Pat Ament in 1976 presented me with a surprise first draft of a book about my climbing activities, I was delighted. For here was an exceptional writing talent who also was an innovative and inspiring boulderer—a combination of attributes unique in my experience. When Pat first coined the phrase "the poetry of mountaineering," it was apparent that he had a deep appreciation for the less obvious.

Pat is also a spiritual warrior and a wonderful poet, a karate expert of many years standing, as well as one of the very best climbers of his generation—one who laid the foundation for future rock climbing. In this broad sense, he is both unique and accomplished—a paragon of American climbing.

Pat Ament at Gem Lake, late 1960's, photo by John Gill

John Gill at Split Rocks, Colorado, early 1960's

The Solitude Of Mastery

John Gill became known throughout the rock climbing community of America in the early 1960's for the sheer side of a thirty-foot spire, the Thimble, in the Black Hills of South Dakota. Word of this achievement, an overhanging wall done above a guardrail and without a rope, reached climbers. Some dismissed this as a bouldering stunt. Others, such as Royal Robbins, recognized the efforts of a master spirit.

For years after the ascent of the Thimble, Gill would continue to capture the awe of climbers, his name spreading throughout the world, as he set the standard for bouldering difficulty wherever he went. His physical prowess included the ability to do a one-arm pull-up from only one finger. Stories characterized Gill as a quiet soul who seemed to defy the pull of gravity and, almost more important, who defied the pull of vanity—a man with a stately voice and dignity, yet who never presumed that his activities deserved notice in the mainstream of climbing. Gill in fact was shunned by some in the late 1950's and early '60s. The limited mentality of Mountaineers and big-wall climbers of that era often equated greatness only with size. As they saw it, theirs were higher heights. They tended to dismiss bouldering as anything important. Indeed the scope of Gill's climbing consisted largely of smaller boulders or obscure solo climbs in the Tetons.

At the peak of his form, and many years before the majority of climbers could comprehend his talent and level of ability, Gill pursued his goals in relative solitude, mastering these short rock faces, "boulder problems," and training himself toward the far edge of human, physical capabilities.

Along with his rational and earnest cultivation of gymnastic strength, Gill clearly possessed a natural physical gift. Another climber trying to follow every step of Gill's training might fall far short of Gill's performance on rock. As with great artistry, it was impossible for Gill to be the subject of imitation. Even super-star climbers today only tentatively assume they approach Gill's level of mastery. Those assumptions are shattered by attempting some of Gill's more difficult routes and by remembering that he did them by himself, without the influence of a community of competitors, when there were no sticky-rubber shoes, and not the peer inspiration that exists today. Gill's consciousness matured at a time when the consciousness of climbers in general was embryonic.

Yet the consciousness of bouldering always was, for Gill, rooted in the joyful, simple creativity of play. His achievements have been a blend of physical and intellectual activity that deepen, upon reflection, to subtle (sometimes witty) espousals of philosophy. Critical to that philosophy has been a strong appreciation of nature, solitude, sky, streams, wildlife, different colors of the rock, hills delicately in bloom, and forests and air....

Gill's Parents

John's mother, Bernice Alman Gill, was a traditional southern belle—resilient, honest, known for her integrity—from an authentic southern family that went back several generations and could be traced to the pilgrims. His father, John Paul Gill, was a mathematics instructor at the University of Alabama, one of seven children who grew up in the small coal-mining community of Warrior Run in Pennsylvania.

Gill's father, born in 1910, worked his way through high school—an accomplishment comparable to getting through college today. He worked in a mine during the week, taking care of horses that pulled the carts. Deep in the mine was a small stable in which the horses lived, and he fed and watered them while studying his high school lessons throughout the night by lantern. He became valedictorian at his high school. He gave his money to his mother to save for him, and she set it aside so that he would have money for college. John senior was the only member of his family who went to college: a year at Penn State and then to the warmer climate of the University of Alabama. He completed his degree while supporting himself as a campus cop. Pursuing his master's degree, he met his wife-to-be, Bernice Alman, who also was a student (a "cotton top," as she described herself) at the University of Alabama. She took a mathematics class from him. Not long after, they were married.

Boy With Dogs And Alligators For Friends

John Paul Gill Jr. was born February 16, 1937, in Tuscaloosa, Alabama. As a fourth-grader in Tuscaloosa, Gill lived with his parents in the country in a small, garage apartment in the middle of a large field. He walked to school, along a forest path. Through these woods, going and coming, especially coming back in the afternoon, he began to develop a feeling for solitude in the outdoors. Several friendly dogs that lived near his house came and met him every afternoon in the forest as he returned home, his first outdoor companions.

The family moved to Houston, Texas, and lived for two years in a suburb called Galena Park. A creek flowed through a wooded lot and through a culvert under the road about two houses from John's. He sometimes looked into the culvert, or shined a light down it, and on occasion saw a couple of large, red eyes staring back at him. He and friends thought this was a large bullfrog and threw things into the culvert or let things drift down, in hopes of a response. Eventually a heavy rain flooded the culvert and washed up an eight-foot alligator. All in all, John preferred the friendly Tuscaloosa dogs as outdoor companions.

During the summer, walking down a dirt road that bordered a wooded park about half a mile or so from where Gill lived, he encountered large ponderosa pines. There was sunshine, light striking the forest floor, and pine needles lying around. Within a block, approximately twenty sizable timber rattlesnakes, curled up, were basking in the heat.

John senior decided to get a Ph.D. in economic statistics and enrolled at the University of Texas in Austin. The young Gill went to an Austin elementary school and then to a junior high school. After class, in a playing field near the junior high, by a stream, he and a few others met on a regular basis with a couple of black students who weren't allowed to attend this school at the time. Gill enjoyed playing football and baseball with these friends.

Buildering and Loft Climbing, Gill's First Ascents

At age twelve, with no serious objective in mind, John started scrambling on the walls and pillars around the campus of the University of Texas. It seemed adventurous and exciting, until campus security chased him off. He and his parents then moved to Florida where his father took a job as a young assistant professor at Florida State University in Tallahassee. They lived in the country, surrounded by wooded farmland, where John and his friends taunted bulls—then ran to a barn and climbed to the loft.

Catching Sharks

As a boy, in the late 1940's, Gill spent many summers with his grandparents, William and Annie Alman, at their home in Gulfport, Mississippi. He reminisces about these times:

"My room above the front porch had a series of windows along the front side, facing south—toward the ocean several blocks away. I would lie in bed reading Ellery Queen, Thorne Smith, Kipling, and others until one or two in the morning, a soft, cool breeze coming through the open windows. Sometimes late at night, thunder-storms rolled in off the Gulf with wild, shrieking winds, rain or hail, and crashing thunder.

"I loved to fish in the Gulf. I would rise at 5 a.m. and walk to the large shipping harbor, buy a half pound of fishing-shrimp, and spend the early morning casting my line into the ocean. I fished in the afternoons when it appeared that a storm was moving in. Casting into the rising breakers, I could catch peculiar fish driven in toward land by the approaching weather—weird creatures I was reluctant to cook or eat.

"When I was twelve, I was possessed by the idea of catching a shark. The harbor was deep and the water a dark, almost opaque green. I didn't know what quiet giants cruised its depths, but I had once seen a large alligator gar—perhaps two hundred pounds—that was taken there. Tales existed of huge hammerheads. I

bought a thin nylon rope and a giant metal hook (several inches long) with an evil barb on its tip. Cane grew in my grandparents' yard, and I cut a six-foot long, two-inch diameter, piece for my pole. I then cut a section of a two-by-four for a float and took a large nut from Granddad's workshop for a weight. In the early morning, I bicycled out to the harbor, as far out as I could along one side of it, to a series of large pilings spaced every four feet or so and rising eight feet out of the water. At one time, these had supported a pier. There were only a few planks left, and I was forced to jump from one to the other to get to the outermost. I baited my hook with a freshly caught fish, tossed my heavy line in, and sat down on one of the posts, ready for whatever might come. The waters were still, and I was far out on a peninsula—well away from others.

"After a wait of twenty minutes or so, my wooden block slipped below the surface. I pulled at the pole. It was like trying to stop a submarine. The float reappeared, movement stopped, and I realized I was in over my head. I quickly detached the rope from the pole and tied it around the solid piling I straddled. There, that was more secure. Let's see what happens. Very slowly, the float sank beneath the surface again. The line played out this time at a steady pace and became taut, pulling against my perch. The piling began moving. I scrambled to my feet and jumped to the next piling, barely keeping my balance. When my former post reached a forty-five degree angle, the rope broke. My tackle drifted off into the harbor, vanishing beneath the surface, then reappearing some distance away, until it was finally gone.

"At a different area, at a landing for swimmers reached by a lengthy pier, I swam with porpoises in shallow, translucent waters. You couldn't see the porpoises, but what a thrill when they brushed up against you.

"Granddad had a tiny grocery store and gas pump

about a block from the beach. I worked part-time as a clerk and eagerly awaited Thursdays when the new comics would come in. I would carefully read of the latest adventures of the Spirit, and of the Blackhawks, and that great American hero the Fighting Yank.

"There was a small resort and medical clinic across a vacant lot from my grandfather's store, and the owners had a large, fierce-looking Doberman named Midnight. Midnight had a black Scotty companion, and for some strange reason these two would get out every night about eleven or so. Sometimes I would sneak out and meet these two wonderful creatures, and we would race through the night—down quiet, residential streets that were softly illuminated by a full moon and lampposts, breezes off the Gulf stirring bamboo leaves and the high crests of oaks.

"In 1951, when I was fourteen, I would sneak down the stairs of my grandparents' house at midnight, out the back door, and across to the garage where granddad kept his new black Dodge with Fluid Drive. I would stealthily open the large doors and push the heavy car out into the alley, then wait for a steam engine locomotive that was always faithfully on schedule. The engine would pass by two blocks away, and sleepers accustomed to the rhythms of the tracks would never hear a car being started. I would drive up and down the coastal highway for fifteen or twenty minutes, then quietly drive the car back into the garage and close and lock the doors. (When I was a father many years later, I would sometimes check the odometer of my own car in the evening and on the following morning.)

"Other images from Gulfport, Mississippi.... I recall listening attentively to a seaman who was staying at my grandparents' house. He told me stories of his wartime adventures and gave me a genuine steel knife from his ship's mess, a utensil I later honed to a razor's

edge and hid away. Slipping one day into a boarded-up, decaying antebellum mansion, expecting to find only dust and cobwebs, I instead was startled by post-Civil War decor untouched for many years—velvet drapes and chandelier, faded Persian rugs, and a trunk full of clothing—including a confederate uniform and sword. The mansion was blown into splinters by hurricane Camille twenty years later."

"Unathletic Son" Excels At Climbing

In 1952, Gill's father accepted a teaching position at the University of Georgia in downtown Atlanta. As a junior in high school, in 1953, Gill was enticed into climbing by a friend, Jeannie Shearer (later the secretary of the American Alpine Club for several years), who spoke of Indian treasure lost for centuries in the wooded and rolling mountains of northern Georgia. According to an intriguing legend (described by an archaeologist in an article in the *Atlanta Constitution*), a cave could be found in Fort Mountain at the southern end of the Appalachians. The cave's entrance, hidden midway up a set of forested limestone cliffs (the Beehive Cliffs), was marked by a carved turkey-claw. A small group of friends packed sandwiches and a nylon rope and set off toward the fabled cliffs. For footwear, Gill wore floppy, high-top basketball shoes.

The treasure they discovered was "the primordial appeal of climbing on steep rock, stimulated by exposure"—as Gill later would write. The scent of mountain laurels was in the air. Lichen skittered down the gray limestone face as they moved from hold to hold. It was an activity so astoundingly different from traditional southern pastimes that it was next to impossible to discuss their experiences with parents and peers.

John visited north Georgia on several more occasions,

including a few trips with his father. As John climbed, his father belayed the rope. John's father was supportive but uneasy about this radical new activity his previously unathletic son so liked.

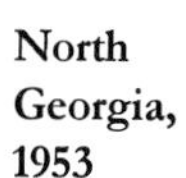

North Georgia, 1953

North Georgia, Cloudland Canyon, 1954

11

Fort Mountain, North Georgia

After graduating from high school, Gill and Dick Wimer, one of John's friends from the little Georgia climbing group, planned a trip west to the bigger mountains of Colorado. Dick had climbed in Rocky Mountain National Park and wanted to return. John's father later admitted to John—to the amusement of them both—that he took out a burial policy on his adventurous offspring!

So in 1954, Dick Wimer and Gill drove out from Atlanta in a convertible "Model A" to climb and hike in the mountains of Colorado. The car had non-hydraulic brakes, and Gill found it electrifying when he first took the wheel on a precipitous mountain highway.

They were joined by another friend in Boulder and teamed for an ascent of the Maiden. Here Gill, at age seventeen, had his first taste of legitimate rock climbing. He became the middleman of a three-man ascent of the standard route up the Maiden and was fascinated if not somewhat intimidated by the exposure of the magnificent free-rappel from the spire's summit. They also did the thirteen hundred-foot Third Flatiron above Boulder, then drove to Estes Park and to Meeker Park where they camped.

Gill had been told of the popular Longs Peak, rising into the cold, high altitude a few miles north of their camp. He wanted to climb the mountain via the formidable, two thousand foot, granite East Face. Dick had broken his leg on Longs the previous year, wasn't ready to go back, and did not feel good about Gill trying it. But John wanted a real mountain experience and informed his partner that he was going to do the climb the next day. The seventeen-year-old Gill got up in the morning at 4 o'clock and hitchhiked to the road leading to the Longs Peak campground. The weather looked suitable. He walked the six steep miles to the base of the East Face, having in the way of gear a fifty-foot length of manila rope, an ice-axe, and his first climbing shoes—J.C. Higgins workboots. He had put on the boots the type of lug rubber soles that mountain climbers used in those days.

13

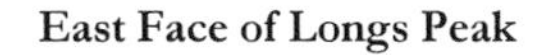

East Face of Longs Peak

The route he chose started up the left side of the face, on the Mill's Glacier buttress. His skills were unpolished, but the thrill of exploration was overwhelming—setting his whole body vibrating with energy. In a steep couloir, he suddenly arrived at what appeared to be an impasse. Seeing a knob of rock above, he doubled his rope and threw it up. It caught on the knob, and he pulled himself hand over hand past this obstacle! In a state of intense excitement, he arrived at Broadway—the large ledge halfway up the wall. He was awed by the sweeping verticality of the Diamond—the upper, right-hand portion of the east wall. At that time, climbers questioned whether the thousand-foot Diamond ever would be scaled. *The Window Route*, to the left of the Diamond, had only just been done.

It appeared suddenly that another climber was coming up to Broadway from below, so Gill waited. The other person arrived, dressed in an alpine outfit with knickers, a little cap, and heavy sweater. He introduced himself as Al Hazel, a local mountain guide. Al said that he was scheduled to replace the summit register and had planned to go up the easy *Cables Route*, or via the keyhole. But he had spoken with Bob Frossen—the Longs Peak head ranger—and learned that Gill was up there by himself. Frossen was furious. People weren't supposed to do that sort of thing. So Hazel had agreed to take a look. From a high point on the trail, he was able to spot Gill.

The two talked for a few minutes, and the guide saw that Gill wasn't simply a wild teenager seeking thrills, that Gill had some idea of what he was doing and where he was going. They continued up as a team and, using Gill's fifty-foot rope, tied together for part of the upper portion of the climb. The summit register was replaced, and they started down the *Cables Route*. Hazel had a painful trick knee that went out, and Gill's ice axe served, fortunately, as a cane for the many slow miles back to civilization.

As they approached the ranger station, the guide said, "You wait here, I better clear the way for you." He went down and talked to the ranger. After about fifteen minutes, he returned and said, "O.K., you can come down." He gave Gill a ride back to the campground where Dick Wimer was angry that John had gone ahead and done such a serious climb alone. Wimer referred to him sarcastically as "twinkletoes," an appellation Gill shrugged off.

Tensions subsided after two or three days, and they decided in fact to climb the peak together via the *Cables Route.*

Following this ascent, they managed a number of other classic peaks in the park and also went to the Maroon Bells—an isolated and lovely area at the time. There were only two other people at Mirror Lake when Gill and Wimer ascended the Bells via a traditional route during August of 1954.

15

Gill at the summit of Longs Peak, on a later occasion (after an ascent of the *Cables Route*)

Rambling Wreck

During the fall of 1954, Gill enrolled at Georgia Tech and became "a rambling wreck from Georgia Tech" who drank his whisky clear, as the song goes. He was "irrevocably hooked on rock climbing" and investigated the campus for climbing possibilities.

He borrowed his father's car and with a friend drove several times up to Cloudland Canyon, in remote north Georgia, to explore and climb on the canyon walls. Although a state park, there were few people if any around during the fall and spring. On their first trip here, Gill rappelled down into the canyon, some distance away from the camping area, over a hundred-foot cliff and into brush and dense woods. As he stood next to the wall, he heard movement and caught a glimpse of a jacket and glint of steel. He didn't need to think it over. He hurried along the base of the cliff until he found a break in the wall where he could scramble rapidly up a chimney and back to the top. He and his friend looked over the edge but could see no one. The next morning at daybreak, and approaching the cliffs, they saw several wisps of smoke rising from the dense forest below. They judiciously found another set of cliffs to climb, in a side canyon.

John later talked with an old, retired state ranger who said that the smoke was from illegal moonshine stills. If in the vicinity of the smoke one dropped a bucket on a rope over the edge of the cliff, with five dollars in the bucket, a tug would be felt after a few minutes. Lifting the bucket out would bring the moonshine purchase. The old ranger added, "If you go into the woods near the stills, you will be shot and killed." Shades of *Deliverance*.

Gill leading at Cloudland Canyon, 1954

As a freshman at Tech, Gill was required to take three physical education courses. The most formidable of these was swimming, where Fred Lanoue—who had taught naval aviators to survive under critical conditions—required students to become "drown-proof." A swimmer's hands and feet were bound (hands behind the back). The student had then to jump into the deep end of the pool and swim back and forth across the pool without touching the walls or the bottom. After undergoing this ordeal, Gill showed only "modest talent" in the second course: track. He ran a tremendous 440, pulling away from the pack early, but fell exhausted twenty feet from the finish line. Even after a summer of hiking and climbing, he had not learned to pace himself and exhibited an impulsiveness that later would occasionally put him in precarious positions in rock climbing.

Gymnastics, the third course, appealed to him because of its possible application to climbing. He had a flair for certain pulling exercises, the most notable being the twenty-foot rope climb—starting in a sitting position with the legs extended and using only arms to ascend.

Once or twice a week, after studying until about 10:30 or 11:00 in the evening, he and a friend crawled stealthily up various buildings and other structures of the Georgia Tech campus. Gill was beginning to use gymnastic chalk for climbing and used it on these buildings. A particular night in 1955, they climbed to the top of a slender, overhanging light tower on the football stadium. They then lowered their army surplus, nylon rappel rope to the distant parking lot below, and John began to rappel. Halfway down the rappel, the approaching headlights of a campus patrol car illuminated the roadway not far away. Quickly pulling up the rope and holding it in his lap, Gill hung silently in the shadows, turning gently in a soft breeze, as the vehicle crept past directly below.

The evening prior to a nationally broadcasted football game, the two darkly-clothed climbers strung a line between two light towers and in the middle of the line hung a gigantic piece of paper with a huge eye painted on it. A fad, going through the undergraduate culture, had to do with a mysterious, threatening, phantom eye.

They climbed on the administration building, a Victorian structure with nooks and crannies, little towers, and odd projections. It was somewhat scary, because portions of the building were treacherously unstable. They had an excellent time on these outings, often coming back at about 12:30 or 1:00 in the morning.

Forty Foot Slide To The Bottom

The second year at Georgia Tech, in 1955 and '56, Gill had become a member of a fraternity and, while living in the fraternity house, introduced a couple of other people to climbing. They went out on Saturdays to Stone Mountain, a seven hundred-foot granite monolith in the woodlands near Atlanta. Neither he nor his two best fraternity friends had a car at the time, so they rented bicycles and rode to Stone Mountain. Considerable effort was required to get there and back, because of the hilly terrain, but adventure and fun far outweighed the exertions of the journey. At the finish of a day's climbing, they bicycled to a restaurant along the highway, had a steak dinner, huge glasses of ice tea, and arrived back at the fraternity house at about two hours before midnight.

Cables and scaffolding from a partially completed Confederate memorial on the vertical north face of Stone Mountain swayed gently overhead as he and friends worked on short, technical face climbs at the bottom of the wall. While climbing, they could hear the rusty girders of the memorial creak, swaying back and forth, in the wind. It was the only sound except for the wind in the trees. Gill remembers being astounded to find a Holubar piton lying on a ledge below the large, silent, granite soldiers. "It was hard to imagine other climbers in Georgia in the mid '50s."

On one of his early visits to Stone Mountain, still wearing basketball shoes, he bandoliered a rope around his chest and started to lead up gradually steepening rock. There was considerable lichen, and the rock was smooth. He climbed to the steepest point, lost frictional contact, and slid forty feet back to the bottom, skinning his chin and fingers and putting a rough finish on his new nylon rope.

John and his dad hiked around Stone Mountain together on several occasions. The area then was peacefully devoid of people, unlike the carnival atmosphere of today. In the clear, cool Georgia fall, under a deep blue sky, they scared the foxes out of holes, studied eagles and hawks, and picked wild grapes that grew among the rocky outcrops.

First Visit To The Black Hills, Tetons, And Estes Park

During his stay at Georgia Tech, John took a long trip with his parents. They made a one-day stopover at Devil's Lake, Wisconsin, John's first visit to this area. Here he discovered Cleopatra's Needle and soloed a route up it. He also soloed *Weissner's Face*. They drove through the Black Hills of South Dakota. At the Needles area, where there were hundreds of small pinnacles of rock, he got out of the car and soloed a couple of easy spires. It was exciting. They also visited the majestic Teton range of Wyoming. Gill wanted to climb one of the Tetons and met several members of the Princeton Mountaineering Club who were planning to go up the east face of Teewinot the next day. He joined with them, climbed Teewinot, and then he and his parents drove to Colorado where he scrambled around on some crags near McGreggor Rock in Rocky Mountain National Park.

Speed Rope Climbing And Gymnastics

As a member of the Georgia Tech gymnastics team for a brief time, Gill performed the speed rope-climbing event. Don Perry, a rope-climbing inspiration during the 1950's, had set a speed record of 2.8 seconds for twenty feet—faster than most people could pull a loose rope on the floor between their legs. Gill's fastest unofficial time, attained after he had left Tech, was 3.4 seconds. Besides Perry, Gill was taken with the great Russian gymnast Albert Azaryin. At Leow's Grand Theater in downtown Atlanta—site of the premier of *Gone With The Wind*—Gill saw a newsreel of a still-ring routine performed by Albert Azaryin and envisioned translating such strength to rock climbing. He immediately became especially fond of the rings and worked both flying and still-rings for a number of years. Not afraid to take a calculated risk, Gill performed the dangerous cut-and-catch on the front swing of the flying rings. He also executed the flying cross.

He transferred to the University of Georgia after two years, preferring its mathematics program, and joined the Air Force R.O.T.C. No gymnastics team existed at the University of Georgia, but apparatus were available to John and several gymnastic friends.

Chalk, Its First Use In Climbing

In '56, he got a summer job for two months with the forest service in Bend, Oregon, establishing "P"-lines for road surveys, laying out boundary lines for timber sales, clearing brush, burning slash, and pruning trees. He climbed several mountains while in Oregon, including Mount Thielson by the *South Face*, wearing basketball shoes. He then took a bus to the Tetons and climbed for about three weeks.

Gill saw serious Teton rock climbers for the first time

on the Jenny Lake boulders, people such as Dick Emerson, Richard Pownall, and Willi Unsoeld. Emerson was a ranger at the time, Pownall and Unsoeld guides. Gill noticed them putting forest duff—the powdery residue on the base of the forest—on their hands to dry their hands before they started up the rock. He realized at this point that gymnastic chalk was indeed the ideal thing. He started using it consistently, introducing it to east and west coast climbers who were in the Tetons.

Occasionally pulling from his pocket a piece of chalk to rub on his hands, he climbed the north face of Teewinot with a friend, the north face of Cloudveil Dome, a number of other longer Teton climbs, and a few isolated rock climbs of modest severity.

Gill on Hangover Pinnacle, in the Tetons, 1957

In 1957, Bob Toepel hiked up with Gill to the base of Symmetry Spire in the Tetons to camp and climb the direct *Jensen Ridge* the following morning. They hoped to climb something else the same day. They built a small fire in a hollow about thirty feet from the only standing timber in the vicinity—an old snag about twenty feet tall. The next morning, they carefully dowsed the remnants of their tiny fire and began the ascent—which at the time was one of the hardest standard climbs in the Park, 5.8 perhaps. They used goldline rope, pitons, and wore Zillertal lightweight rock boots that were very good for edging but poor for friction.

John led up a couple hundred feet, over a large overhang near the bottom of the ridge, and was belaying Bob up. John occasionally glanced at the beautiful, blue sky and fleecy clouds. Suddenly he noticed a wisp of smoke coming from the large tree. Bob reached his position. As they both stared at the towering hulk, it burst into a magnificent ball of flame. They were speechless with shock. Gill recalls,

"There was a biblical grandeur about the fiercely burning, solitary tree, poised like an alpine beacon on the barren, windswept ridge below our perch. We rappelled down and set about making sure the fire could not spread—an unlikely scenario, since we were close to timberline and there was no vegetation nearby. We could only speculate that our small fire the evening before had ignited an underground root system that smoldered through the night before finally reaching the old tree.

"As we cleaned up the ground, Bob spied two figures hiking up the slope below us. As they got closer, we could see they were two park rangers with minimal fire gear. Few words were exchanged, as all of us proceeded to eliminate any lingering fire danger. I had previous experience doing this, since I had worked on forest fires for the Forest Service. We packed up, descended to the boat dock, and caught a ride back across Jenny Lake. As

the excursion boat rocked along, spray flying in our faces, Jewel T., one of the two rangers, informed us we were due at a hearing before a federal magistrate in Jackson that afternoon.

"Jewel was a notorious enemy of climbers, and it was our bad luck that he had taken a hand in this affair. We later drove to Jackson behind the park service vehicle which, surprisingly, parked in front of a small, fishing-tackle shop. The proprietor of the shop was an elderly gentleman with gray hair and mustache who wore a plaid flannel shirt and a western string tie. This was the federal magistrate. He led us into a small back room and cleared away from a table some fishing tackle he had been repairing. We sat down, and federal court was in session. Jewel T., as expected, presented the government's case—slanted in such a way that we appeared to be scurrilous scoundrels bent on burning down the national park. He kept referring to 'the forest fire' and the 'destruction of valuable timber,' at which points I—acting as our attorney—would object strenuously to the prejudicial and false description of this very minor, isolated incident.

"At the hearing's end, the magistrate found us guilty of some form of careless fire making and fined us a minimal amount, $75, if I remember. He saw through Jewel's presentation and, I would guess, suspected some degree of bad blood between us. He also was aware that Bob and I had done most of the work cleaning up. He eliminated court costs and saved us a little. Afterwards, as we strolled out of the shop, Jewel turned to me and said, 'I hope you have a pleasant time in your stay in the park.'"

Cowboy Country

One of the summers John climbed in the Tetons, he hitched a ride into Jackson with his steamer trunk full of clothing and climbing equipment. He rented a tent frame only a block or two from the town square and was given an old bell-type alarm clock and several thick, patchwork quilts, since the evenings were quite cold. Jackson still had at that time a somewhat "authentic" appearance, as opposed to its current cosmopolitan ambience (jetliners circling). The Hollywood movie *Shane* had recently been filmed in Jackson Hole. In the '50s, a stage ran from Jackson Hole to Rock Springs. This was an old, '40s bus driven by a cowboy who looked like Gary Cooper. In the morning, Gill caught the stage. Halfway to Rock Springs, a cowboy passenger got drunk and became belligerent. The driver stopped the bus, pulled the character off, dumped him on the ground, got back in, and drove off—all without saying a word. John Wayne, where are you today?

Athens, Georgia, 1957

America's First 5.10 Routes

John graduated from the University of Georgia in 1958, with a degree in mathematics, and received a commission in the Air Force. He was scheduled to report to the University of Chicago in October of the following fall in order to participate in a twelve-month sequence of courses in meteorology. This would prepare him to serve as a weather officer. But he had a free summer before this educational commitment was to begin and so worked for a month, then spent a month climbing in the Tetons. He explored the buttresses of Garnet Canyon and succeeded at twelve or thirteen probable first ascents. These were formations anywhere from 200 feet to 800 or 900 feet in length.

Gill camped and bouldered with Yvon Chouinard in 1958 and swears he saw a bird commit suicide in Yvon's three-day old dishwater. The bird took a drink and then collapsed.

Gill "rediscovered" Baxter's Pinnacle in the Tetons. It had been climbed with direct-aid by Baxter and a party from Stanford in the mid-'40s but had been considered "lost" for a number of years. He told Chouinard about his discovery, and Yvon and a friend did the second ascent with a step or two of direct-aid. Gill and a companion then climbed the spire free. John and another companion later returned to Baxter's Pinnacle and did a difficult variation, "up the left face of the direct-aid crack." This was a vertical face for fifteen feet or so and perhaps the earliest 5.10 in the country—a degree of severity that had not yet been invented anywhere else in America at the time! It might be pointed out that some of the hardest of these pitches were "optional" (contrived at points where other choices were available).

John did the first ascent of *Delicate Arete*, 5.9 or 5.10 (via the optional line Gill took). What made this route scary was its relative lack of protection at a critical section. Also making the second ascent of the route, with Ritner Walling, Gill got into trouble doing a hard optional move thirty or forty feet above an expansion bolt. A strong wind came up and buffeted him around severely. He had to plaster himself against the rock while on tiny holds. Ritner later described Gill as looking like an ant trying to keep from being blown off by the wind. The wind would cease, and Gill would start to make a move, but all of a sudden he would be blasted by another enormous gust. It would become calm again, and he would start to move, but he was blasted again from a different direction. The worst lasted a matter of minutes but seemed like an eternity. On those tiny footholds, he was using a pair of early climbing shoes that were good for edging but had no real frictional characteristics. These "Zillertals," from Austria, with hard, black, lug rubber soles, were the "state of the art" in rock shoes at the time.

Chouinard speaks about Gill:

"A handful of people were climbing intensively in the Tetons and lived there the whole summer, scrounging on fifty cents a day, eating oatmeal.... At that time, Gill was doing some climbs on Disappointment Peak. After grabbing whatever climbing partner he could find, he'd do some little arete that often wouldn't lead anywhere, because Disappointment Peak is just a big flat thing on top. Kamps and I did Satisfaction Buttress, and it was the hardest climb in the Tetons when we did it, yet the American Alpine Journal refused to publish anything about it because it didn't have a summit. That was where climbing was, in those days. If it didn't have a summit, you really didn't do a climb. Gill was getting even more ridiculous and was doing things just for the sake of pure climbing, going nowhere. These were absurd climbs, as far as the Alpine Club was concerned. Now people do a one-pitch climb, and it's a route, so I guess he was ahead of his time in that respect.

"When a party would go to repeat a route Gill had given a 5.8 or 5.9 rating they would find it to be 5.5, because Gill had done some

unlikely variation which they could not discover. He wouldn't do the most logical way. He'd go out and enjoy himself on hard problems.

"I did a couple routes with him on...the Knob? These were several-pitch, roped climbs. At that time, he was a smooth climber, always under control. But he didn't seem to be a bold climber. There are some people who are extremely bold who aren't exceptional physical climbers, but boldness gets them up the climb. Maybe Gill didn't need to be bold then. He used to do a lot of roped leads, although I don't think he ever really cared for it. He enjoyed bouldering much more and, I believe, was happier when he realized that. It may have tended to make him a bit insecure that everyone else was climbing with a rope. He chose to specialize in one form of climbing, pure bouldering and, specifically, overhanging face climbing. He loved overhangs. He never really got into crack climbing.

"Gill and I developed some of the climbs on the boulders in the Tetons. We named the boulders and worked on them for hours at a time. Falling Ant Slab was named because the angle was such that ants would go up, reach a point, and peel off. There was a route called 'Cutfinger' where you had to use a hold that would...cut your finger. There were sharp quartz crystals, and you'd come back from a day of bouldering with your hands in shreds. That's why we called one boulder Red Cross Rock. I could do pretty many of the climbs in those days, but three or four I didn't have a chance with. He had well over a foot reach on me. The only things I used to get him on were occasional no-hands routes. I had a much lower center of gravity. But when I first bouldered with Gill, he was nowhere as good as a few years later. He was getting better very fast.

"We wrote a little guidebook to the Jenny Lake boulders. Gill did the drawings for it and the gradings of the routes. I wrote the text. It's a classic. The rangers have the one copy and guard it. We wrote it tongue in cheek and patterned it after the guide to the Tetons which says, 'These mountains are big mountains, they make their own weather.' We wrote the same about the boulders: 'These are big boulders, they make their own weather.' We talked about the north faces and the big south faces.

"We'd take visiting climbers to the boulders on rainy days and show them the routes."

Gill on Cutfinger Rock, in the Tetons

Cutfinger, no-hands route

***No-Hands Variation*, Falling Ant Slab ("The exposure is great, a feeling that you'll fall and slide down the hill and into the lake")**

Chouinard continues,

"Gill and I would go together to Blacktail Butte. It is gray limestone, absolutely 90 degrees, all finger holds. I remember the third route he did there. It may have been one of the first 5.10 routes in the country, because that was about 1959 or so. It's one of those things where you've got to go quickly and you've got to conserve strength. Your forearms get pumped up. Of course he didn't have to go fast, because his arms never gave out."

Blacktail Butte, 1959

One-Finger Pull-Up

September 1958, Gill was exploring the lower part of the Thimble overhang, in the Needles, with Fred Wright spotting. A car pulled into the parking lot, a door slammed, and a man fuming with indignation yelled, "Get down off that rock!" Gill replied, "Mind your own business," and continued to climb. The man returned to his car and yelled at his wife, "They're a couple of teenagers looking for thrills!"

During John's year at the University of Chicago, he worked out with the University of Chicago gymnastics team and got to where he could do a one-arm, one-finger pull-up! He worked on this as the result of a rumor. Helmut Rohrl, a German mathematician who lived in Chicago and climbed with Gill on occasion, informed John that Hermann Buhl—the great European mountaineer—was able to do a one-finger pull-up. In those days, people tended to exaggerate the abilities of their heroes. Gill found it to be a provocative idea. He had already developed a strong one-arm pull-up and in no time added this "finesse"—as he called it.

Chalk At Devil's Lake

Chalk on difficult-looking rock faces began to be the mark for other climbers that John Gill had paid a visit.

While stationed in Chicago in 1959, Gill drove five or six times to Devil's Lake—a rock climbing area in Wisconsin. He led or made free-solo first ascents of several routes, including *Sometime Crack* (done solo, 5.10), *Gill Crack* (5.9+), and *Congratulations* (done solo, 5.9). He free-soloed several other routes, including *Ironmonger's Crack* and *Ironmonger's Direct*, and did some bouldering... the Little Flatiron, Gill's Nose, and the Tombstone. John found chalk useful here because of the slick quartzite, especially during the summer when it was humid.

An early visit to Devil's Lake, Wisconsin (1959)

***Gill's Crack*, Devil's Lake (route climbed in 1959, photo taken later—about 1964**

Tombstone (top) and *Leaning Tower* (bottom), Devil's Lake

Next page, clockwise, starting with photo at upper right:
1) *Congratulation Crack*, 2) same, 3) *Flatiron*, 4) *Direct Route*
5) *Ironmonger's Crack Direct*, 6) *Sometime Crack*, "5.10"

(climbs done in 1959, photos taken later in about 1964)

The *Center Route* On Red Cross Rock

In 1959, he finished his meteorology training at the University of Chicago and, in the month or so before reporting to Glasgow Air Force Base in northeastern Montana, drove to the Tetons with all his possessions in a Studebaker Power Hawk. He spent several weeks climbing there in late summer, often sneaking up to do a long, covert solo, an activity that was strictly illegal in Grand Teton National Park at the time.

In the Tetons in 1959, he did the first ascent of the *Center Route* on Red Cross Rock—an exceptionally difficult, short problem and the first significant "dynamic route" in America (if not anywhere). Normally climbs were done "statically," whereby each move was deliberate and often reversible. Gill was willing to commit himself almost to flight, sometimes throwing his body free of the rock and upward off a hold. This route on Red Cross Rock remains to this day a formidable test piece. John would repeat it many times during the years that followed the first ascent.

Center Route on Red Cross Rock (photo taken later in 1965)

Weather Forecaster

By the late '50s, Gill had become the author of countless small, preposterously demanding (however obscure) routes, little incidents of climbing that later would be viewed by the climbing populace as developments far beyond the measure of difficulty anywhere else at the time.

Things got a little dull as a weather forecaster at Glasgow. John would walk up into the control tower during evening shifts and do pull-ups to pass the time. At the base gymnasium, he kept up his gymnastics. He had purchased a speed-climbing rope and a set of rings and hung them in the gym. He worked out for one to two hours, every other day.

Gill wore a gun sometimes in Glasgow, a .22 magnum Colt Buntline with 9-inch barrel. This was legal at the time. It was not allowed that it be concealed, however. One day in 1960 while walking in downtown Glasgow, Gill's best friend, the Air Police commander, saw one of his airmen strolling down the sidewalk sporting two pearl-handled six-guns. Gill's friend discovered that the airman was working as a hired gun for a local rancher and was involved in a ranching feud with the hired guns of another rancher. A couple men had already been shot. A little of the Old West was still alive in northern Montana in 1960.

While stationed at Glasgow in 1960, Gill visited the Tetons and soloed the 5.10 crux move on the north face route of Baxter's Pinnacle, a route that had recently been free climbed by Royal Robbins and companions. Gill adds,

"A guide and a climbing ranger arrived during my climb. They were impressed and a little uncertain about what attitude to take, since soloing was strictly prohibited at the time. An awkward moment ended amiably."

John's solo activities in the Tetons during this time included several routes on the south face of Storm Point and several ascents on the north wall of Garnet Canyon, where he had established a number of roped climbs.

During this summer of 1960, while in the Tetons, Gill met a young Army Sergeant, Mike Borghoff. Mike was in the U.S. Rangers and a martial arts devotee. He was a toughened veteran with several years service and regaled Gill with stories of quick bloodshed and reprisals. Gill says about Borghoff,

"He was the first combat-hardened warrior-poet I had met. I had begun writing a little poetry myself, to fill up the hours at my lonely military outpost on the Canadian border, and I made a deal with Mike: I would teach him the art of bouldering, and he would critique my poetry. Unfortunately we tried to do both at the same time. Mike's verse was heavily laced with images of strength and bearing ('...the young lieutenant's spine, stiff as a rod of steel...') and mine, I'm afraid, was overly sentimental. We gave up after an hour at the boulders, since the good sergeant kept laughing himself off the rock."

During his three years at Glasgow, Gill climbed near Zortman, Montana, on steep, limestone slabs of an area called the Little Rockies.

Steep, limestone slabs near Zortman

The location of an Indian reservation, Zortman was remote and a little wild—the inhabitants unpredictable. Every week or so, one would read of violence. Thus Gill carried his side arm. He would leave the regular roadway and drive his Studebaker Power Hawk several miles across empty prairie to the base of the limestone cliffs. The first time he did this, he stopped beside a gravel road and walked about a hundred yards into a bordering field to check the surface of the ground. An old car pulled diagonally in front of his, and two tough-looking Indians, hard and grim men in their thirties, got out and started walking toward him. One carried a tire iron. Gill was uneasy about this. There was no sign of anyone else for miles, and an Indian had burned down a small schoolhouse the previous week. There was a fair amount of hostility between the Anglos and the Indians. Gill stood his ground and stared at them. They stopped when they noticed he was armed. They stared back for about ten seconds, then turned without a word and walked back to their car, got in, and drove away.

Nearly Lost In The Hourglass

Some of the limestone cliffs that Gill found in Montana were unstable. On one trip, he soloed a hundred feet up an inside corner to the obscure, small entrance to a cave. With flashlight, he crouched and crawled inside and found himself in a large, roughly circular, dome-shaped room, perhaps thirty feet in diameter, with a ceiling some twenty feet above a peculiar sandy floor sinking down in its center. As he moved across the soft floor, it started shifting—funneling into a vortex at the center. It was like walking on the top sandy surface of an hourglass. He moved quickly to the wall and climbed onto a small ledge, listening to a distant rumble as sand and debris vanished into the hole. After a few minutes, the floor ceased its movement. He crept gingerly around to the entrance and crawled out. Indiana Jones, you should have been there.

John sometimes drove down to Fort Peck Dam in good weather, rappelled down into the dry causeway, remaining out of sight of the caretaker's cabin, and climbed up steep concrete slabs to a point where he could ascend a short overhang and up a vertical wall to the top. The solitude was magnificent, the terrain bleak but attractive. Warm Chinook winds melted the snow in spring, and in the drying air "the brown hills seemed to breathe." During the winter, and bundled in a wolf-fur parka, he ice-skated along the Milk River, barren trees overhanging the frozen streambed.

Frisbee Throwing With Garbage-Can Lids

Dave Rearick recalls John visiting the Tetons:

"In August, 1960, I spent two or three weeks in the Tetons, at the climbers' campground on the south shore of Jenny Lake which the rangers had created a year or two earlier to try to keep the climbing scene out of the sight of the general public. There's no trace of that campground anymore, except maybe the old kilns that Yvon Chouinard and Ken Weeks were sleeping in, or the big tree in the clearing where one night somebody, likely the Vulgarians, lassoed a bear and pulled him down with a rope attached to a truck. And perhaps the large cement slab of unknown origin is still there, on which for several hours every morning John Gill and I practiced our hand-balancing. John was able to do a 'stiff-stiff' body press, and I kept working on it. I got a little closer every day with encouragement from John, but never quite succeeded, until finally, right after he left and there was no one to show off for, I did five of them in a row.

"For lunch we'd go over to the little general store run by two old ladies and try to absorb as much protein as possible. John favored a thick, pasty mixture of powdered milk as a good muscle-builder, never mind what it tasted like. Afternoons, we had long sessions of hatchet throwing, along with Bill Woodruff who had bicycled across from Yosemite and was resting

up before riding further east.

"Later on, John would usually drive over to Blacktail Butte for an hour or two of solo climbing. I never accompanied him there, and few people knew just what he was up to, but Bob Kamps went along once or twice and later told me he couldn't top-rope some of the things John was soloing. As for the little boulders around the campground, there was none, even if only knee-high, that had not felt the tread of John's tightly-laced climbing shoes on whatever tiny crystals or minute features it offered by way of a bouldering problem.

"John Gill was a frequent visitor at the Jenny Lake Ranger Station, usually not to sign out for a climb but to practice fingertip front levers on the doorjamb. From the parking lot, all you could see was a pair of long legs extending horizontally out the front door, knees together and toes carefully pointed.

"All of his exercises, from the most outrageous bouldering maneuvers down to his Frisbee throwing with garbage-can lids, were executed with the utmost control and painstaking attention to style. All of this, together with his agreeable manner and a certain intriguing reluctance to separate reality from absurdity, made John an outstanding companion for whiling away those long, exuberant summer days."

Gill doing his "front lever"

The Daunting Thimble Route—The First 5.12

During the late '50s and early '60s, Gill soloed a number of climbs in the Needles—occasionally putting up a new route in the process. His solo ascents included Spire One, Spire Two, Khayyam Spire, Spire Four, the Wicked Picket, the Incisor, Inner and Outer Outlet, the Gnomon, the Kingpin, Flying Buttress lower variation, Pinnacle variations, and others. Some routes had bouldering starts. John recalls,

"Difficulty ranged from 5.2 to 5.12, and I enjoyed the easier climbs every bit as much as the harder ones. Sometimes I took a rope along and self-belayed, and other times I free-soloed, taking only a rappel rope."

This experience in the Needles culminated in a most amazing ascent. In the spring of 1961, Gill did the first ascent of the sheer side of the Thimble, a thirty-foot pinnacle in the Needles. This route brought the first real fame to Gill, although he was never seeking fame. The sheer, extremely difficult ascent was done without the use of a rope or any form of protection, completely solo, and risking a fall onto a parking lot guardrail.

On an earlier visit to the Needles, in 1960, Gill had climbed the Thimble via another route that followed a faint groove on the left side of the east wall. He then began to consider a line up the steeper face to the right. He "scrambled" halfway up the groove route to look over at the holds on the steeper wall. It became apparent what sorts of moves he would be responsible for if he were willing to commit himself to such a climb. He felt that it was time he do something more committing, with more of an element of risk, than the relatively safe (however difficult) boulder routes he enjoyed. Yet he did not feel that the route of which he was thinking was a suicide mission. There was a "possible escape" halfway up where he might, if necessary, move left to the groove.

With an image in mind of this unclimbed, overhanging wall of the Thimble, John returned to Glasgow Air Force Base and started to devise ways, around the gym, in which to train for some of the moves that he anticipated doing. He squeezed nuts and bolts sticking out of the gym walls to prepare for the nubbins that he would have to squeeze high up on the Thimble. He could do seven regular one-arm pull-ups, three fingertip one-arm pull-ups, and of course his one-finger/one-arm pull-up, and he continued to train at these.

The Thimble remained on his mind during the winter, and he returned to it on leaves from the base. His approach was to climb up and down the bottom half of the route until he had that much wired. Once or twice, he jumped from a high point. He had developed skill at leaping from high places, as related by Richard Goldstone in regard to a different climb:

"Gill jumped off from about twenty feet up and landed like a cat in the midst of jagged talus boulders."

At last Gill worked himself "into such a fevered pitch" on the Thimble that he committed himself to the top portion of the route and, as he admitted, "very fortunately made it."

He would state later in an interview,

"You not only get psyched up but almost become hypnotized or mesmerized to the point where your mind goes blank, and you climb by well-cultivated instincts. You do it."

John can't recall if a young airman named Higgins accompanied him on that culminating trip to the Needles. Higgins at least had served as a spotter for Gill during an earlier look at the Thimble.

Having reached the top, knowing it was over, and in a world by himself, Gill felt "a peculiar absence of feeling." He said little about the route, before or after. He did not brag.

The start of the difficult route on the Thimble
(photo taken of Gill Several years after first ascent)

The Thimble (dotted lines indicate Gill routes, the most difficult route to the right)

At first, when Gill's bouldering in the Tetons and in the Black Hills became known, it was believed by some that such routes had no intrinsic importance. Size, elevation, and glorious summits were more in the spirit of the mainstream focus at the time. Many climbers in the late '50s and early '60s did not want to recognize bouldering, even when they became aware of it. It was easier to believe that these routes were stunts rather than extreme artistry. Gill's routes in fact were the actions of a private, humble, but nevertheless inwardly competitive individual who had more or less invented his own medium. Also—because of Gill's solitude and private approach—much of what he accomplished remained relatively unknown. There were tales around campfires of some kind of mythical person who had mastered an overhanging wall in the Needles or who had done a few difficult solo ascents in Wyoming's Tetons. Gill relates the following story:

"I was once bouldering in solitude in the Needles, when a young female climber walked up and introduced herself and asked who I was. I told her and continued bouldering. She turned and walked away after a few minutes, saying over her shoulder, 'You can't be John Gill. He climbs much better than that.'"

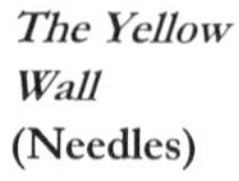

The Yellow Wall **(Needles)**

Gill on his route on the *Direct North Overhang* of the Scab

Paydirt Pinnacle, *Southwest Face Direct* in the Needles, mid-1960's

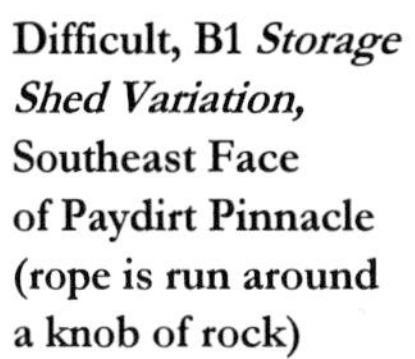

Difficult, B1 *Storage Shed Variation,* Southeast Face of Paydirt Pinnacle (rope is run around a knob of rock)

Outlet Boulder

"Hard variation" of *the Yellow Wall*, Sylvan Lake Boulder, The Needles

The Spike, after the first ascent, 1964 / Rachael, after the first ascent, 1963

Molar, first ascent (5.9+), 1966 / Ropeless on Stumbling Block

Hagermeister Boulders

While the woman in the Needles did not believe John was *the* John Gill, at other instances there was no mistaking that one was in the presence of Gill—as in the following account by Paul Mayrose:

"This is a tale of a first encounter—stereotyped perhaps, but quite real nevertheless—with John Gill. Bouldering was a new concept around Estes Park, Colorado, in the early 1960's. None of us locals were quite sure how to approach it. It could be entertaining, but should it ever be taken seriously? The answer put in an appearance one pleasant Saturday afternoon.

"It was the Hagermeister boulders. I don't remember the cast of characters. Bob Bradley was certainly there, Dave Rearick almost certainly... and perhaps half a dozen others. A person was introduced as John Gill. Mr. Gill was a tall person, quiet, and not particularly impressive physically as long as he stood absolutely still! If he moved in the slightest, he rippled and bulged. I decided that he was healthy.

"As the afternoon progressed, so did most of us. Ah, the competitive instinct! Gill got quite far enough off the ground to convince me that bouldering was not any kind of sop for frustrated acrophobiacs. His funny business enabled the rest of us to climb better... without getting overly philosophical.

"He climbed, and I watched. He climbed, and we fell off in his wake... in droves. Eventually I became convinced that he wasn't actually strong enough to cheat by gouging his own holds into the rock. A few of the cast became discouraged and left. Others and I got mad and determined and stayed... and started getting up occasional things we would not have recognized as climbable that morning.

Gill on *Fenton's Corner* at the Hagermeister Boulders, early 1960's

"Bouldering had come to Estes Park in earnest. Basic concepts hadn't been changed, but the order of magnitude certainly had. I took up bouldering. For me it was never an end in itself, but it became the difference between 5.8 and 5.9 (even a little 5.10) on bigger climbs. As always, advance stemmed from one individual who pushed beyond convention. A committee of 5.9 climbers cannot meet and climb 5.10 or anything but 5.9. But one man can. John Gill showed me that levels of climbing could be pushed higher. Knowing him, I went in search of my own limit. Apparently I found it, but I have never since tried to guess the upper bounds for someone else. Not bloody well likely after the shock of a first meeting with Gill."

Hagermeister boulders (about 1962)

Gill repeating Dave Rearick's painful Hagermeister *Hand-Crack*, "without jamming!"

Gill's hardest route at the Hagermeister boulders

Near Gem Lake Trail, Estes Park

Bread Loaf,"
near start of Gem Lake Trail,
near Estes Park
(photo taken later, about 1967,
with daughter Pam)

"Hard problem" off Gem Lake Trail

Routes near Gem Lake Trail

Near Estes ("A hard route. My belayer went off belay to take the photo, while I clung there.")

First ascent (solo) of Rat's Tooth on Twin Owls, above Estes Park

Angel Overhang, near Estes Park

Moraine Boulder, on the road to Bear Lake, west of Estes Park

One of Gill's hardest routes at Split Rocks,
Between Lyons and Estes Park, Colorado, 1961 or '62

The Delicate Wall, Split Rocks

Not Just A Show Of Strength

In the course of his one-arm, one-finger pull-up training, Gill developed the ability to do it also on the middle finger of his left hand and on the index finger of his right hand! A one-finger pull-up set a certain gauge of strength, a most severe task for even the strongest, flyweight gymnasts. Approaching a hundred and ninety pounds and six-foot-two, Gill had no such advantage of lightness. This element of size made his accomplishments all the more impressive.

Skeptics suggested that Gill was all muscle, a show of strength. But at the Jenny Lake boulders in the Tetons, a number of competent climbers found it difficult to repeat—with the use of all four limbs—some of Gill's no-hands routes. With phenomenal balance and footwork, he "walked" up steep faces of rock. There was no question for anyone who spent time with Gill that his footwork, balance, creativity, problem-solving insight, subtlety, and control were commensurate with his strength.

The Bayonet, in the Needles (Gill notes, "I spent thirty minutes working out a way to face climb the crack. Then Ray Shragg followed, without a thought about using the crack entirely.")

Impressions From the Needles

A brief characterization of Gill is offered by Bob Kamps:

"In the Needles in the '60s, I found Gill to be a little aloof or cold. But I can only recall bits and pieces. I remember that Gill drove a little sports car. There was a short, leaning face, which Gill was able to climb by starting atop a small, round piece of wood. With this cheater's stick, he was able to reach the first holds of the route. But he wouldn't allow me the use of a ten-foot log to stand on."

Paul Piana speaks of Gill's presence in the Needles:

"A walk through the Needles would be a relaxing joy suddenly shattered when one of our troupe would spy a tiny, white arrow pointing up an overhanging bulge or smooth slab. The idea that they were drawn in jest faded as we learned more about Gill. We made an ascent of the Thimble's easy side. The summit register said, 'Hats off to John Gill,' signed by Royal Robbins. Gill had done the overhanging side of the rock, to Royal's and everyone's amazement. A trip to the Spire 1 area gave us our first glimpse of Gill. He was high up, alone on the spire. It was the first solo ascent of the route. Renn Fenton showed us a boulder problem, a smooth, flared, upside-down trough with an arrow, and said that even when Gill strained you didn't know it."

Marriage

When Gill left the Air Force in May of 1962, he packed up all his belongings in a VW sedan he'd purchased in Glasgow and left the base for a summer of climbing and hiking before starting graduate school at the University of Alabama. He drove first to Zion National Park, where he did some climbing and bouldering, then stopped at several places in Colorado. In

Colorado, he made several solo ascents, including a route on McGreggor Rock in Estes Park. This route was difficult, in stiff Klettershue.

John ended up in the Tetons where he met his wife-to-be, Lora, in the climbing campground. It was early in the season, and Lora and John were the only people there for several days.

John slept in an old-fashioned, Wenzel umbrella tent pitched beneath a tree. Every morning at about five a.m., a squirrel dropped remnants of a pinecone down on the tent, and Gill would drowsily beat the canvas sides. Then the squirrel jumped from a limb three or four feet above the top of the tent onto one side of the tent and slid down it like a slide. It became a regular thing, like nature's alarm clock. Here was another of Gill's outdoor companions.

Lora and John left the Tetons, went to the Black Hills, enjoyed some climbing together, journeyed to Colorado toward the end of this summer of '62, and were married in a magistrate's office in Boulder.

The two then drove to Alabama to Gill's parents' house in Tuscaloosa where they stayed until they could get a downtown apartment in an old antebellum home. John watched many hours of *Rocky & Bullwinkle* between studies and brewed sake in a tub in the kitchen closet—until the landlady found out.

Alabama

John returned to graduate school to get a master's degree in mathematics at the University of Alabama. He continued gymnastics on his own and found good bouldering in northern Alabama, at locations such as Shades Mountain (outside of Birmingham) and Desoto Canyon. There were even a few climbing spots around Tuscaloosa, deep in the mossy woods on cement-like conglomerate with huge pebbles.

Shades Mountain, Alabama

Shades Mountain, Alabama

"In 1963, I am a beginning climber at Devil's Lake, Wisconsin, and experienced climbers tell engrossing stories around the campfires. The name John Gill is attached to tales of a person able to do one-arm pull-ups while pinching the 2x4's of a basement ceiling. Gill seems to possess more of the qualities of heroic myth than of flesh and blood. Yet climbs at Devil's Lake are there to prove the myths: Gill's Corner, Gill's Crack, Sometime Crack, The Flatiron....

"In August of 1964, my brother and I are in the Tetons contemplating the underside of Red Cross Rock—a twelve-or-so-foot, mushroom-shaped boulder. Two figures wander over to us, and we recognize Rich Goldstone whom we know from Devil's Lake. We exchange greetings, and Rich introduces us to his companion, John Gill. Dave and I nearly faint, for we've half-believed that Gill had no corporeal existence. We observe, as the two climbers use mysterious white chemicals on their fingers, mats for their feet, and tiny lichen brushes while devising extreme routes up the boulder.

"Finally Gill moves to the north corner overhang, stands on a small foothold, grabs an undercling with his left hand, and reaches with the other hand out over the bulge for what appears to be nothing. He simultaneously springs and does a one-arm, fingertip pull-up on this nothing. Dave and I fail to comprehend what we have seen and, after the two leave, examine that hold. It is about an eighth of an inch wide."

Rearick's Challenge

Among the colorful west were many kinds of personalities, nonconformists, and medicine shows—the traveling salesman, the Bohemian, the male-gorgon characters of American society.... With these perhaps should be associated the traveling boulderer, a lone aberration, or oddity, of the larger world of mountaineering. The loner was John Gill, who made brief visits to little areas of boulders across the country (and disappeared away from them as quickly like a chimera). He was a law unto himself, outlandishly unique—especially in that he was so solitary. Yet he was not unsociable.

Climbers knew him and liked him. They may not altogether have liked the way he reduced them to beginners on the boulders, but they liked him.

In 1963, Dave Rearick had found some bouldering possibilities just west of the town of Estes Park. One rock featured a steep, shallow groove above an overhang. Rearick speculated that this route would never be done. Gill took this as a challenge and climbed the route.

Rearick's Challenge, **just west of Estes Park**

John made a mysterious visit or two to the Shawangunks of New York in about 1964 and did a number of "eliminates" there. A handful of eastern climbers at the time tried everything from karate yells to shoulder stands in determined efforts to succeed. No one did.

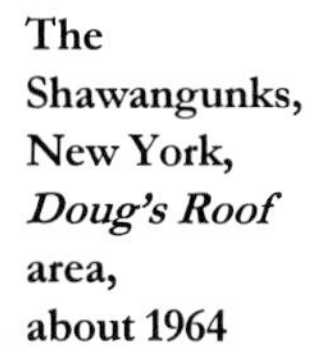

The Shawangunks, New York, *Doug's Roof* area, about 1964

Perhaps in anticipation that other climbers might want to attempt his routes, Gill sometimes drew chalk arrows on the rock—indicating the start and general line of ascent, or pointing to some high hold that was the goal. Climbers who began to be followers of Gill looked for these arrows. There were certain artistic, and sometimes hidden or subtle, ways in which these arrows were drawn.

Keyhole, the Shawangunks

The Shawangunks, Brat (*Gill Variation*) / "Gill's Egg" (originally done 1965)

In 1964, legendary Yosemite climber Royal Robbins visited the Needles of South Dakota and tried to repeat Gill's Thimble route. Royal was unsuccessful and was very impressed with the style of Gill's ascent—no top-roping beforehand to get the route "wired." Robbins wrote in the summit register, "Hats off to John Gill."

When Royal visited Boulder, Colorado, I (Pat Ament) became his main climbing partner. We went to Castle Rock. Royal had heard that Gill had done something or other at Castle Rock, so we looked for what seemed like any possibility. We noticed a slightly overhanging, short wall with a thin, finger crack running up through it. Gill must have climbed this, and it became our desire to repeat the route. As Royal was leading, a car drove slowly by. We heard the frail voice of an elderly woman in the back seat of the car. She called to us, "That must really be the final exam." When Royal and I realized that the route had much lichen and no signs of Gill chalk, we claimed it as a first ascent and named it *the Final Exam.* Gill would visit Castle Rock later, in 1968, and by coincidence free solo *the Final Exam (*now rated 5.11c, although perhaps 5.10 c or d for a taller person*).* Gill also established, in free solo style, Castle Rock's impressive bouldering test piece *Acrobat Overhang* and the short but intense *Gill Crack.*

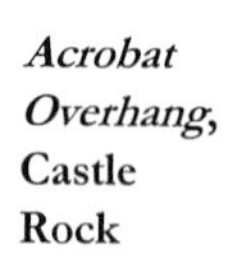

Acrobat Overhang, **Castle Rock**

Free solo on the *Final Exam*, Boulder Canyon, mid-1960's

Royal Robbins and John Gill were the two best climbers in America through the mid-1960's. Royal's bold spirit gravitated toward John's, and sometimes it was the other way around. Gill sometimes repeated routes Royal pioneered.

Gill leads second ascent of Royal's Queenpin in the Needles, about 1965

It would distort the nature of Gill's climbing to label him "only a boulderer," as was done sometimes through the 1960's. He often led roped climbs and certainly made solo ascents that were high off the ground (sometimes many pitches in length).

Triconi Nail, the Needles mid-1960's

**5.10 route on Inner Outlet Boulder,
Needles of South Dakota,
photo taken 1965**

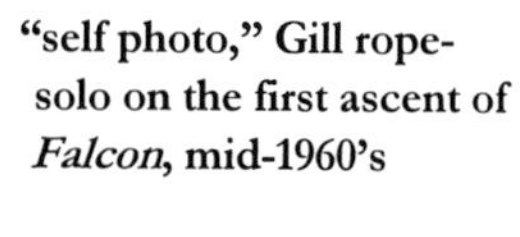

**"self photo," Gill rope-
solo on the first ascent of
Falcon, mid-1960's**

Climbing In The South

Their second year in Alabama, Lora and John moved to a Tuscaloosa housing development for students. Barracks had been converted into apartments at the site of an old naval base. And although not a particularly attractive place to live, they had the bare necessities. This complex would be blown up later in 1977 as part of the filming of the Burt Reynolds movie *Hooper*. Gill was delighted to see the very place he had lived go up in smoke.

When Gill finished his master's, they moved to Murray, Kentucky, where their daughter, Pam, was born in 1965. John met several Persians who became his friends and taught him how to play soccer.

Murray, Kentucky

In 1965, Gill found Elephant Rocks in Missouri. These big, round granite boulders were somewhat devoid of holds. Yet Gill scratched a way to their tops, defeating the impossible-looking.

Elephant Rocks, Missouri

Short rock climbs and bouldering were to be found in Southern Illinois, at Dixon Springs and in Kentucky at Pennirile Forest State Park. John put up several difficult boulder routes at Dixon Springs, including *Rebuttal*—a smooth, bulging, sandstone wall fifteen feet high. Cave-In Rock State Park, on the Ohio River, and Bell Smith Springs were two other areas John visited.

Dixon Springs, *the Bulge*

"A hard route," Dixon Springs

Ship's Prow, Dixon Springs

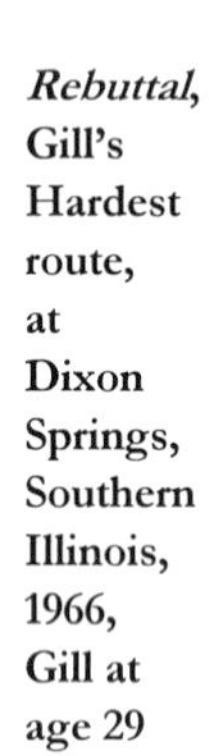

Rebuttal, Gill's Hardest route, at Dixon Springs, Southern Illinois, 1966, Gill at age 29

Dixon Springs

("A challenging solo")

Jumbo, Dixon Springs

Pennirile Forest, Kentucky

A *Hidden Overhang*, Dixon Springs

Persian Wall, Dixon Springs

Persian Wall, Dixon Springs

Bell Smith Springs, Southern Illinois

Ray Shragg, Rich Goldstone, and R.F. Williams, climbing friends of Gill's who were living in Chicago, drove down to visit him for the Christmas holidays, 1965. It turned extremely cold, but they were determined to climb. They drove in Gill's VW bus to Dixon Springs and bouldered in several inches of snow, in bright sunlight. It was about five degrees above zero. They drove to Cave-In Rock, bouldered a bit until their fingers were almost frostbitten, then took a ferry back across the Ohio, stalling for an hour in mid-river due to impacted ice in the river. Gill's bus had a dinky heater, which did nothing to dispel the intense cold. Rich kept saying, "I can't believe we drove all the way down here to climb in this weather." It took hours for them to warm up back at Gill's small apartment near the campus of Murray State.

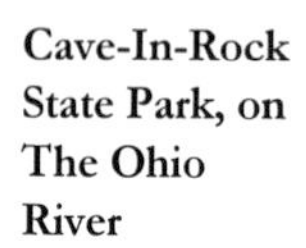

Cave-In-Rock State Park, on The Ohio River

Gill speaks about R.F. Williams, a math and climbing friend who put himself through grad school as a dancer and who now is a leading mathematician:

"Bob almost bought it in the mid-1960's [1966] when he and I were doing the first free-solo, no-hands climb of the sixty-foot Needle in Estes Park, Colorado. He was coming down from the top when the piton hammer in his pocket caught on a rock and threw him almost off an overhang. He stayed utterly calm. I think I was more distressed than Bob."

Gill (left) and R.F. Williams,
first no-hands ascent of the Needle, near Estes Park, 1966

Rich Goldstone

"I Recall My RDs Slipping A Bit"

One of Gill's more well known boulders, the Outlet Boulder in the Needles, has a story that John relates:

"Pete Cleveland and I worked on this problem one afternoon in about 1967, and he was ahead of me and almost had it, when I discovered a quick dynamic move that would put me up it. At one point in our struggles, Pete flew off onto the flat ground on his back in a cloud of dust and lay there, stretched out, panting, and spinning some colorful language."

Gill recalls about Pete Cleveland,

"Pete was a fierce, highly skilled competitor and the gutsiest lead climber I knew. I watched as he did an outstanding, unprotected first ascent on one of the Ten Pins, creeping to the top on tiny nubbins—any one of which could have popped off. He was nerveless.

"On the Flying Buttress Variation (5.11) in the mid-sixties, several others tried unsuccessfully to repeat

the pitch I had done (which is probably much easier now in sticky shoes). When I did it, it was a hot humid day. I recall my RDs slipping a bit on the easy, sloping rock above the pitch. I quickly made it to the crack extending below the prominent chimney and down-climbed what then became the standard start for the larger climb. I walked up one day to find Pete contemplating the harder variation, not in the best of moods. I demonstrated the technique I had used, and he was able then to make the second ascent. He continued roped to the top of the spire to do the entire climb in his usual, impeccable style."

First ascent of the *Flying Buttress Variation*, 1967

In 1967, Gill visited City of Rocks in Idaho and established the first hard routes there. Very little climbing had been done in the area at the time.

City of Rocks

Below: Difficult sequence at City of Rocks

The Move To Colorado

In 1967, Gill decided to get a Ph.D. in mathematics. He wanted a school that was near a climbing area, and Colorado seemed an appropriate place. He applied to both the University of Colorado in Boulder and Colorado State University in Fort Collins and liked the offer he received to be a graduate teaching assistant at C.S.U. He never would regret this choice.

Gill began to climb with a student and university gymnast by the name of Rich Borgman. Just before being kicked out of the gymnastics room because he wasn't a team member, Gill was told by the gymnastics coach that there was a climber "who could crawl all over the walls without any visible holds." This piqued Gill's curiosity. The two finally met and climbed together extensively on the solid, yellow-brown, Dakota sandstone running along ridges near Horsetooth Reservoir west of Fort Collins.

Rich Borgman at Fort Collins

One-arm pull-up training

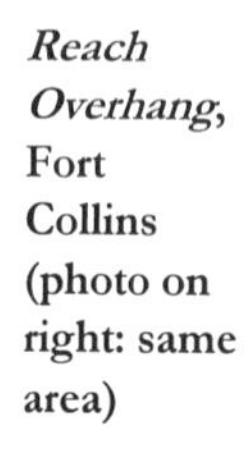

Reach Overhang, Fort Collins (photo on right: same area)

Bouldering a typical roof at the road-cut area

Sunshine Boulder, Fort Collins, Colorado (photo taken about 1969)

Harder route on Sunshine Boulder

Difficult roof-face below *Torture Chamber* area

Left Eliminator, 1968 (looking south)

Left Eliminator (looking north), photo taken later, in 1973

The one-finger pull-up

Right Eliminator

Overhang at Dixon Dam, Fort Collins

"near south end of reservoir"

First ascents of *Center* and *Pinch Overhang* on Mental Block, "A very cold day, maybe 20 degrees"

Hard variation: traverse from *Pinch Overhang* to *Center Route*, then up

Mental Block, *Left Side*

Center Route on Mental Block, later unroped ascent

No bouldering of any real difficulty had been done at Fort Collins, and John put up dozens of routes. Among his Fort Collins routes were: the *Eliminator Left Side, the Eliminator Right Side*, the Mental Block via *Pinch Overhang* (and other Mental Block routes). His *True Torture Chamber* exercise was a traverse of 5.12 or perhaps 5.13 difficulty.

I (Pat Ament) had heard of Gill as far back as the early '60s and on a climbing trip to the Needles of South Dakota had seen his route, his turning of the soul, the Thimble. Skeptics who had put Gill down as a "only a boulderer" were of little consequence in light of one very positive soul who pursued his personal goals, cognizant of, but undisturbed by, the views of others. It must have been something to behold—if anyone was there to watch—Gill's strength and balance approaching their limits, hands tightening, feet edging ingeniously on fragile pebbles.... I hoped one day to meet him and climb with him.

In 1967, I was a gymnast at the University of Colorado. I was the only other person using chalk in climbing. Chalk bags did not exist yet, and I placed a small block of it in a pocket or sometimes held the block in my mouth so that my fingertips could find it quickly. I was setting a few standards of my own on boulders of Flagstaff Mountain, just above Boulder. In a letter to me a year earlier, in 1966, Royal Robbins wrote, "Sounds as if your strength and gymnastic ability are formidable. You should soon step into Gill's shoes as the boulder king of the U.S." This never would occur, but for a time I would perhaps be one of the three best boulderers in Colorado, which included Gill and Borgman. And we would be considered by some the three best in the country.

It was exciting when I learned that John was in Fort Collins. I phoned him, and he invited me to join him for some bouldering west of Fort Collins at Horsetooth Reservoir. I arrived at a small trailer where he and his wife lived with their young daughter Pam. At the boulders, John and I joined by Rich Borgman. I recall John sailing upward from the ground to a high finger-hold, as he ascended *the Right Eliminator*.

Below roadcut, Fort Collins

After doing a few problems, I mistimed a dynamic reach. Because my body was completely elongated, as I reached backward on an overhang, I was unable to get my feet under me and fell more or less with a straight body. I landed with the full force of my weight on a sharp talus boulder, the point of impact an inch or so above my tailbone. The result was an amazing shock to my entire body, although miraculously I was unhurt. Step into Gill's shoes? He expressed genuine concern and was relieved to find that I was not injured seriously. Shaky, I continued in the role of observer for the remainder of the bouldering session and watched Gill and Rich climb overhang after overhang.

To my surprise, I soon competed against Rich in a gymnastic meet in Fort Collins between the University of Colorado and Colorado State University.

Gill one day took me to Split Rocks, a wonderful garden of boulders located on a forest hillside approximately twenty miles northwest of Boulder. I had bouldered here before, and once with Royal Robbins, but never with John. Low and commanding, his voice was rarely heard except for an occasional deep chuckle in response to my exertions. He approached a smooth, overhanging, fifteen-foot wall of a boulder and, at first, gently drew breath. Then his eyes became fixed upon a high hold. While compressing his upper torso, as if to recoil, he began to breathe rapidly. To follow was a perfectly calculated, slow motion leap. There was a subtle, although important, shuffling of his feet on tiny nubbins. One hand reached over the rounded summit, the other pulled laterally. It was quick, and he was at the top of the boulder. I squeezed the initial holds and sighed. I could grasp the holds but not the problem.

Gill tried to dispel my romantic notions, insisting that he had lots of weaknesses and that I was the real climber because I did longer routes and big-wall ascents. We rigged a top-rope, and Gill belayed me on the *Delicate Wall.* My first try, I got a hand on the top. But I failed to grab it well.

Gill belays Ament on the *Delicate Wall*, at Split Rocks

Gill on the *Delicate Wall*, Estes Park, Colorado

John and I climbed the better part of a day at Split Rocks. Jagged granite blocks strewn throughout the pines wore the flesh of our fingertips and shredded our egos. A warm sun made the day pleasant, and we invented many sorts of problems. I realized that there was more training in store for me, if I were to repeat a few of the routes that Gill ascended with authority. I looked forward to that training and to returning to this area—which would become my favorite of all bouldering areas. On my next visit to Split Rocks, a few days later, I would make the *Delicate Wall* and would repeat it again and again on subsequent visits. The route seemed to bring Gill to me when he was not there.

John had climbed at Split Rocks for years and done many routes. He showed me quite a few of them, and I directed my efforts to each and all, and to a few I could only speculate might be his.

Gill's *Hand Traverse*, Split Rocks

A finger-tip route, Split Rocks

Split Rocks (a route a bit high off the ground)

High, unprotected face climb at Split Rocks

Strenuous mantel

Hand crack at Split Rocks

Another day, I repeated Gill's route *Acrobat Overhang* at Castle Rock. This was a proud second ascent that I made a point to do in Gill style—without a rope, and no previewing from above.

"So strong and directed is Gill's presence," my friend Tom Higgins noted. Almost in a ghostly way, thoughts of Gill followed me. Even as I watched an issue of the TV series *Star Trek*, Captain Kirk had a confrontation with a certain John Gill—"the Fuhrer."

Trips To Veedauwoo

Between 1967 and '71, Gill would make occasional visits to Veedauwoo, an area of granite across the northern border of Colorado into Wyoming. Many of these boulders were exceptionally round and holdless, or the holds were tiny and painfully sharp.

***Mirror Face*, Veedauwoo, Wyoming**

Hull's Boulder ("Tricky route")

"Direct aid crack," Veedauwoo (a cold wind dictated that Gill use one of his daughter's diapers to shield his ears)

Veedauwoo

Veedauwoo

Veedauwoo ("Really hard route, especially at the start")

Clam Shell, Veedauwoo

Veedauwoo problems

One-Arm Front Lever
And The Art Of Bouldering

The summer of 1969, Gill was climbing around the diving rocks at Dixon Dam on Horsetooth Reservoir. He recalls,

"I usually took a descent route that involved climbing down a face that ended in an overhang, and blindly lowering over the overhanging step to the top of a small pedestal, then to the talus. As I put my foot down and felt for the top of the pedestal, I heard a furious rattling. I jerked my foot up and leaned back to see what was happening. A huge rattlesnake was coiled on the two-foot-square top of the pedestal, rattling at me. It was so upset that it slid over the edge onto the rocks below. After a stunned moment, it slithered off."

***Reach Overhang*, Horsetooth Reservoir, Fort Collins**

Tucked innocuously into the pages of the 1969 American Alpine Journal was Gill's first climbing article, called *The Art Of Bouldering*, wherein he explained that bouldering was not merely practice for longer routes. It was an art in its own right, in the spirit of gymnastic competition: "...the boulderer is concerned with form almost as much as with success and will not feel that he has truly mastered a problem until he can do it gracefully."

In that article, Gill listed a few skills that might be developed by a serious boulderer, including one-arm mantel presses, one-arm pull-ups with a hand squeezing a beam, one-arm fingertip chins on doorjambs, and one-arm/one-finger pull-ups on a bar. As a gymnast, he had learned moves such as the "inverted iron cross" and, also on the still-rings, the slow, straight-body, inverted pull from a hang to a handstand. His favorite ring maneuver was the "butterfly mount," through an L-cross, an exercise beginning with a straight-arm hang and pulling into an iron cross. He pointed out that these skills were not absolutely necessary for bouldering but might add a certain polish to one's climbing!

Climbing indeed was, for Gill, an extension of gymnastics. In his backyard in Fort Collins, Colorado, he set up a few pieces of apparatus for working out. He was able to do a one-arm pull-up while holding his 30-pound daughter and taught himself—perhaps invented—the one arm front-lever, a position where the body is held horizontally in the air while hanging from one virtually straight arm! Gill applied this specific skill to routes at Horsetooth Reservoir that required a kind of extended leverage, with arms out on either side of the body, pressing up on fingertip holds.

This flair for strength simply reduced all his partners to mere observers on certain routes. John had all the qualities to be able to climb certain kinds of rock better than anyone in the world. He had the one-finger pull-up. He had a good, long reach, his being over six feet in height, he had superb footwork and incredibly strong fingers, and he had the one-arm front lever. He also had a good head for the creative solving of problems. I was often surprised at how easy a few of his routes looked at first. I would discover that some wonderful, little, hidden trick of technique was thrown into the mix, along with the need to express a great deal of physical (and mental) power.

One-arm front lever

Roadcut area

Gill noted in his American Alpine Journal article that flying moves, lunges, swinging leaps, and moves where the climber had more or less to fling his body through the air from one hold to another, were not execrable mutations of good technique—as thought by many classical mountaineers. These methods could be disciplined and artistically executed. In addition, they were perfectly valid, as well as logical, techniques for a climber with a flair for acrobatics.

Duncan's Ridge, Fort Collins (rock ripples and back ripples)

Yet Gill's true element was solitude, except for those times when he bouldered with a partner (and even then he cherished the solitude of nature and sharing it with a friend). John kept up his free soloing by doing longer routes on Gray Rock Mountain near Fort Collins. He also soloed routes in Estes Park and several of the shining quartz faces high in the Snowy Range of Wyoming.

He liked to walk about in the woods or through mountain terrain and either avoided busy climbing areas or made himself unseen in such areas. He did not conform to mainstream perspectives but rather was drawn to the expression of his own inclinations in some solitary place that had obscure, indistinct-looking rocks or lost cliffs. Throughout the country, many small, steep surfaces of rock that mattered to no one else consumed him. His mind went to the lone, critical, micro-crystal of rock that was the key to a single move. Yet a typical ten or fifteen-foot high Gill problem, one difficult enough for him to earn his private grading of "B2," would be less attainable for most climbers than the summit of Everest.

Gill in fact was beginning to be accorded the same respect as Walter Bonatti, Hermann Buhl, or Royal Robbins. His celebrity was derived from these very small rock climbs—boulders. From the Shawangunks in New York and the rocks of Devil's Lake, in Wisconsin, to more obscure areas of Alabama or Montana or Missouri, in South Dakota and a host of areas in Wyoming, and throughout Colorado, Gill left a mysterious presence that climbers local to each area respected.

Gill, Boulder, Colorado, 1968

Attempting A Gill Route

The test for an aspiring climbing (or at least a joy) was and still is to repeat (or at least experience) a Gill route.

Steve Wunsch writes about such a try:

'Ever wanted to make an outrageous assertion and get away with it? Just pick the blankest side of a boulder or the most ridiculous looking overhang and say that a few years ago you saw John Gill walk by and climb it. Now if the individual you are trying to 'sandbag' has had the privilege of visiting areas where Gill has climbed, the worst you're likely to meet in the way of skepticism is a wide-eyed 'How?'

'Kevin Bein was disarmingly well prepared for my query ('How?') and responded with a flourishing, carriage-road ballet amply narrated with talk of side-pulls, levers, and swing moves. He almost had me believing it until he had Gill jumping off from several feet above the overhang where Gill thought better of trying to mantel on a pile of sloping, wet leaves. 'Nobody would jump off from up there!' I said.

"'He did. He down-climbed a move first, jumped off, then walked on down to the next problem.' Well, sandbagging is the name of the game in the Shawangunks. So while we were setting up the top-rope I half sensed that I was about to be taken for a ride, and I don't mean up. This supposed climb sported an overhang just as big and about as high as Doug's Roof (indeed it was the same roof but went over just a bit left, where there was no crack). The number of hours and roped falls, which went into the freeing of Doug's Roof, are an embarrassing matter of public record. If Kevin had tried this tale on me using anyone but Gill as its hero I'm sure I would have dismissed it instantly. But the mere mention of Gill's name evokes memories, which seem to establish credence for the wildest of human aspirations. Didn't I try every Sunday one winter to do the left side of the Eliminator at Fort Collins? I eventually got the lunge on that climb down well enough to bloody my left hand consistently on the hold but not hang onto it. I've seen pictures of him doing it without a rope....

"...Or being in the Needle's Eye parking lot digging into my pack for the compass (I never did need it on Ben Nevis) to see if that really

was the Thimble's north face. It was. Or standing under the Red Cross Overhang in the Tetons after years of trying, listening to the drizzle in the forest (I'd never really gotten high enough for rain to matter), thinking of the first bouldering I did in the Tetons, years before, and a bright-eyed, young friend saying with awe, almost whispering, 'Want to see a 5.13 climb?' I did. All modesty aside, I began to realize that this overhang with the rope now dangling down past it might actually go, unbelievable as it had seemed only minutes before. I even fancied that, using slight modifications of Kevin's pantomime, I might do it. I had, however, made some miscalculations as to the sizes of, and distances between, each of the holds and was quickly swinging onto the rope, glad at least of my calculation that 'nobody would jump off from up there.' In fact I didn't get anywhere near the spot Gill jumped off from. Nor, to my satisfaction, did anyone else that day."

Gill As Friend And Inspiration

In 1969, I (Pat Ament) was sitting alone in a deserted Camp 4—the bouldering area of Yosemite. Pine needles were in my climbing shoes, and chalk that I had been rubbing on my fingers was in my hair. The boulders had worn me out after a couple hours of ascending them. A breeze blew through the lofty trees, and I gazed upward at surrounding walls of granite that rose thousands of feet. A waterfall roared in the distance. The Sierra Nevada scene, spring smells, sun, and sky were telling me to look beyond the surface of life. I began to reflect upon bouldering, its loneliness, and its challenges. In the hot afternoon, a drop of sweat in my palm became a crystalline image of John Gill. He was encouraging me to laugh at myself, because I was too serious. I felt the intrigue of a man whose name was blowing softly through the forests of the Grand Tetons, the South Dakota Needles, Colorado, and many areas. I thought of his gentleness, an individual who was kind and who had a warm, astute sense of humor. I felt that the ascents I now was doing on the boulders of Camp 4 could be attributed in part to the time I had spent with Gill. Yet I had my own abilities, a flair for mantels, and one-arm mantels, and for finding footwork to get me up arm-strength problems. I had strong hands. Gill was somewhat at the heart of it all, though, since I thought about him often and viewed him as the top of the standard in most respects. Whenever I wondered if a route was truly worthy, I imagined him and more clearly knew. He and I, along with Rich Borgman and Utah's Greg Lowe, were the most dedicated boulderers in the country at the time.

I repeated the hardest routes in Camp 4, including Chuck Pratt's notorious mantels, and added a few new test pieces of my own. Of course it would not have been honest to feel that I had "bettered" Pratt, since Chuck used no chalk and was making the first ascent of those routes. He, Royal and other Yosemite climbers, such as Barry Bates, Jim Bridwell, and Tom Higgins, continued to command my respect.

After returning to Colorado, I bouldered several times with Gill. On Flagstaff Mountain, he did many of the hardest problems, for example *Smith Overhang*. I demonstrated the route and then, standing on the final mantel shelf at the top, saw his hand appear just below my foot. He was right behind me, moving upward without hesitation. I felt gratified in a small way when he was challenged by (or did not do) at least one or two of my creations, including a one-arm mantel problem and another route in the Flagstaff Amphitheater I viewed as my *Mini-Thimble*. He did not want to attempt the latter of these two because he was unsure of the strength of the small finger pebbles. The landing was a dangerous one. When he asked if these Flagstaff pebbles were any good, I said that they were. At this instant, he pulled a baseball-sized quartz crystal right out of the side of the Pebble Wall and laughed. After a few attempts, he did manage a dynamic ascent of my *Right Side of the Red Wall*.

John's most impressive accomplishment on Flagstaff was a first ascent one day of a route a few steps to the right of *Smith Overhang*, involving a huge, free, aerial swing. Gill literally flew from the ground to a sloping hold very high up near the top of an overhang. I later named this route *the Gill Swing*. It was a route no one would repeat anytime soon, if ever.

In Eldorado Canyon, John on-sighted my *Milton Boulder*. He used a swing move, following a line about a body's width to the left of my line. We spent some time at a boulder (which I named the Gill Boulder) in the far west end of the canyon that had a few routes John had put up even before meeting me. In one burst of amazing skill and strength, he instantly did another new route—up the slightly overhanging center of the west face (the *Center Direct*). The route moved quite high above the ground and had a dangerous landing of sharp, angular boulders.

Gill Boulder, Eldorado Canyon, *Far Right Side* of west face, mid-'60s

Rich Borgman was with us on one of John's visits to Flagstaff and made impressive repeats of a number of difficult routes. It was an interesting quirk that Rich rarely seemed to do first ascents but could repeat almost anything.

Gill brought me one afternoon to a bouldering area along the trail to Gem Lake, near Estes Park, and we pushed our limits again at Split Rocks.

As I climbed alone on Flagstaff countless evenings in the late '60s at the peak of my ability, often with the boulders all to myself, I experienced a few proud, inspired, invincible, moments as the master of my own rock. I had no idea, however, how "momentary" my time in the limelight was to be. Several serious injuries that I would suffer would put an end to the bouldering extremes that I enjoyed.

Injury And "Down-Time"

At Fort Collins, Gill came out to the cliffs with me but was suffering from a severe tendon injury in one of his elbows and did not attempt to climb. Gill's violent and supremely powerful expression of climbing, his mastery of such difficult moves as the "one-arm front lever," and the stress that his great strength placed upon his tendons were beginning to have their physical price.

There were a few routes at Horsetooth that required "a kind of extended leverage," with arms out on either side, pressing up on fingertips—the sort of thing that was facilitated by being able to do an iron cross on the rings. John had cultivated such strength also by developing the one-arm front lever. Perhaps more than anything, the one-arm front lever contributed to the difficulty he now was experiencing with his elbows. For a period of a little over a year, he would have to give up bouldering completely, because he experienced such enormous pain in his elbows—his right elbow in particular.

Even on an easy climb, the pain would become so intense that he would nearly black out. He referred to the problem as "climber's elbow" and later would note,

"It's a little like 'tennis elbow,' except that it's on the inside of the arm as opposed to the outside. It's an inflammation at the point of the attachment of the muscle to the bone, due to severe strain. Or possibly—one can't tell without surgery—the tendon might actually pull away from the bone a little."

Many years later, these words would seem prophetic—when his right bicep would actually become detached from its connecting point at the elbow.

In reality, his muscular strength had exceeded the power of his tendons. Those tendons were not able to withstand his exertions. To relieve the tensions of schoolwork and for physical exercise, he hiked up and down the hills around Horsetooth Reservoir. Climbing could be enjoyed vicariously, by going with Rich Borgman or me up to the bouldering area. John belayed or acted as coach. He one day took me to a forest of hidden boulders west of Horsetooth Reservoir where routes awaited exploration. He showed me one that he'd had his eye on, a *Red, Overhanging Wall*, which I somehow managed to climb my first try. I felt that he gave me the route—since it would have been his. I was in my best physical shape ever, and Gill, although depressed about his elbow, seemed inspired. The frustrations of his injury seemed to diminish with just the thought of climbing.

As Gill began to heal and return to climbing, I badly tore the tendon in the middle finger of my left hand. The tendon was virtually destroyed, and for two years it would be painfully difficult to hang with my left hand from even the largest hold. Then, doing handstand pushups one morning, I experienced a highly debilitating and perhaps permanent injury deep in the core of my right shoulder.

Returning to bouldering again, John was so weak that he could not do five consecutive two-arm pull-ups. A few friends wondered if the days of his bouldering were finished. After difficult months, using his mind as an instrument of healing and wondering if he would climb hard again, he entered the game with a new attitude. He warmed up carefully and for longer periods before attempting anything, to prevent re-injury. He was a little pickier as to choice of routes. And he forcibly controlled the impulse to keep at a problem beyond the familiar point of diminishing returns.

Telekinesis And Levitation

As John returned to his old Horsetooth climbs, he astonished those individuals who were in his company. He was soon able to play at the hardest routes. He found in bouldering sharp, clear reality, and on occasion a feeling that—with the right consciousness—he weighed a little bit less. The right mental attitude might inspire "a slight sensation of telekinesis" or in fact minutely perceivable levitation. It was easy to listen to such concepts, as they flowed subtly and with somewhat of a sense of humor from Gill. After all, he did at times seem to defy gravity.

Bob Williams speaks of his initial impressions of Gill:

"One look at Smith Overhang on Flagstaff in 1969, and I was hooked. Coming from the east with little climbing experience, I had never seen anything that difficult. My dreams were of El Cap, but my true love of bouldering had just begun. Like most climbers, I tried moves statically. Unlike most climbers, I didn't have enough strength. It soon became obvious that Smith's would require lunging, and since I saw even good climbers lunging now and then, I was quick to accept it as semi-legitimate technique. Besides, I really wanted to climb that overhanging piece of rock. I liked dynamic moves, because they allowed me to keep pace with my

contemporaries. In my case, however, I overdid it, and I think many people frowned on my style—it wasn't pretty. Encouraged by Dave Rearick, I decided to seek out John Gill—the undisputed master of dynamic bouldering. I ventured to Fort Collins, hoping to find problems that could only be done with dynamic moves. John and Rich Borgman gave me the grand tour, wonderful problems on wonderful rock. Still, I wasn't prepared for what I saw there.

"At the Right Eliminator, John poised himself at the base with one hand casually placed on a small hold, then hopped from the ground to a good hold high on the route. The Mental Block provided more of these controlled jumps from the ground. It bothered me that he started so many problems this way, no matter that they were quite hard to do. I thought, 'This can't be fair. Why avoid the problem by jumping past it?' Unconcerned with any rules committee, John played by his own rules. He did these jumps simply because they were aesthetically pleasing. He was, of course, capable of very difficult moves both from the ground and well above it. I never became comfortable with this technique, even to this day. At Fort Collins, however, I found more than a mentor. I found my savior."

Bob Williams, at Fort Collins

Pueblo

Lora and John stayed in Fort Collins until 1971. She completed a bachelor's degree in mathematics at Colorado State University, graduating at the same time Gill earned his Ph.D. When John was offered a position as assistant professor of mathematics at the University of Southern Colorado, Lora, Pam, and he moved to Pueblo. In the draws and foothills around Pueblo, John's mental divining rod quickly located excellent bouldering. Before long, Gill had pioneered many routes around Pueblo of an advanced level. Having slowed the pace of his bouldering, he was far from incapacitated.

John met Warren Banks who would become a good friend and bouldering companion. Warren says:

"My initial contact with John Gill was an anxious phone call that I made after receiving information from my Colorado Springs friend Steve Cheney that John was living in Pueblo. John was very cordial and receptive to my expressed interest in climbing with him. Within a week, he invited me to travel with him and his family to Boulder (Flagstaff Mountain) for the day. That day at Flagstaff served not only to permanently redirect my perspective on climbing but also marked the beginning of what would evolve into a very valued friendship.

"During the next couple of years (1971-72), I gratefully and enthusiastically followed John through southern Colorado cactus, scrub oak, and junipers, from one bouldering area to another. John discovered, as well as established, more areas and routes than I would have believed existed in the foothills and canyons in the Pueblo vicinity. Even more incomprehensible is John's ability to ascend these seemingly unclimbable gems once he has located them. Many of the ethereal feats that John accomplished in my presence were the first ascents of what are now considered among the 'classic' front-range test pieces (Ripper Traverse, Little Overhang, the Fatted Calf problems, etc.).

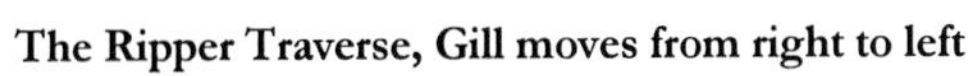
The Ripper Traverse, Gill moves from right to left

"Eagle Move" on the Ripper Traverse

"John also introduced me to a number of other climbing areas, such as Veedauwoo and Horsetooth Reservoir, and to several accomplished, genuinely talented climbers, such as Rich Borgman, Bob Williams, and Pat Ament. Opportunities that John provided me to climb in diverse areas with world-class talent greatly impacted both my ability and motivation. I tend to view my tenure with John as a gift that very few are fortunate enough to receive. While I have experienced the good fortune of climbing with a number of exceptional partners over the last twenty years, none has been more influential to my climbing or personal life than has John Gill! Much has been said, or written, about John's impeccable character. I can only reiterate—he is an absolutely model human being. For an individual to be so nonchalant, particularly in light of so much accomplishment—not only in climbing but also in career and personal life—is truly remarkable."

After two years in Pueblo, Lora and John decided to divorce—agreeing that love was gone. Lora needed to develop her own potential if she ever was going to. It was an uncomplicated divorce, or reasonably so, as such matters go. They filled out the forms themselves, not bothering with an attorney. One of the agreements of the divorce settlement was that, since Lora's future was uncertain, John would keep Pam, even though Lora dearly loved her daughter. Lora wanted to go back to school and wanted to be able to move around from job to job. She lived in Pueblo awhile, attending school at the junior college and also at U.S.C. She lived across town, and Pam divided her time between her mother and father. Then Lora moved to Trinidad, Colorado, where she worked for several months. John put Pam on a bus on weekends. Eventually Lora moved to New York, remarried, and came to work as a computer analyst.

At least one climbing friend of John's speculated that Lora had adopted the negative feelings toward men (and toward marriage) of the "Women's Liberation Movement." Whatever the reason or reasons, the fate of their marriage was sealed. Reflecting in a letter to me (Ament), Gill stated:

"I accept a large part of the responsibility for the failure of our marriage. I was too self-centered, too focused on teaching, and mathematics, and climbing. Not sensitive to her needs. Made career decisions that took us to places having few opportunities for her. I feel guilty about not being a better father to Pam, although I am very proud of her."

One of John's happiest memories is when he told Pam a long adventure story, a continuing saga with a new chapter each evening before bedtime, during the year or so they lived alone. She and he backpacked into the Wind River range in Wyoming and fished for several days, shortly before John and Lora separated.

A New Marriage

John and Pam continued to live in the house that Lora and he had purchased in the Belmont area of Pueblo, below the college.

Dorothy Boggs was a student in one of his intermediate algebra classes in 1973, working at the time toward a respiratory therapy degree. They began dating and were married in Pueblo in 1974. Dorothy had a son, Chris, who was fourteen, and a daughter, Susanne, who was eleven. Pam at the time was nine. John sold his house in Belmont, and Pam and he moved up to Dorothy's house in Colorado Springs. She had been commuting from Colorado Springs, and they lived there for a month while looking around Pueblo for a place of their own. They found an old, attractive house on Third Avenue, a small, two-story dwelling built around the turn of the century. It seemed about the right price, had a certain charm, including pecan floors, and looked as though it would provide enough room for everyone. They sold Dorothy's house and moved into the Third Avenue home where they would stay for eleven years.

Battleship, **"a difficult route hidden in the forest," Pueblo, 1971**

Gill continued to travel and boulder in other areas. Below: A boulder near Lake Marie in the Snowy Range in southern Wyoming, early 1970's

Gill on Beer Barrel Rock, Flagstaff Mountain, Colorado, mid-1970's

"Can You Hold It Right There?"

Middle of winter, 1975, I (Pat Ament) bouldered with Gill in the "badlands" west of Pueblo and found that indeed his injuries were not bothering him too much. He was far from incapacitated. While acutely aware of the possibility of re-injury, he climbed brilliantly. He demonstrated impressive routes he had put up, such as *Little Overhang* and *Ripper Traverse.* I brought a small 16-millimeter movie camera and some black-and-white film. The camera didn't work properly, and would shut off with Gill frozen in mid-flight at some climactic move—at which time he would chuckle as he dropped back to the ground or tried to keep from falling. These moments provided a few laughs and ultimately enough footage to make a short, very rough film that later would prove a bit of a collector's-item.

Fatted Calf Boulder

The most astonishing sequence captured was a route on the Fatted Calf boulder. This involved a dynamic move where John threw himself outward and upward, starting off difficult hand and footholds under an overhang. He then became completely detached from the rock for an instant before grabbing with one hand (at the limit of his reach) a sloping hold at the lip of the overhang. Great stress then tested his hand's friction on the lip as his body swung free from under the overhang. A one-arm pull began the final process of moving over the actual lip.

Free Aerial move on Fatted Calf, Pueblo

One ability of Gill's was to seek out routes that called forth something of the unique powers he possessed, routes that perfectly fit his height, physiology, and particular strengths. Many outstanding climbers began to sojourn to Pueblo to seek out Gill and test their abilities alongside his.

Bob Candelaria summarizes his encounter with Gill:

On the way to one of Gill's bouldering sites, I see that more than the mere physical effort of climbing is required. It takes a gift to actually locate these areas. Observing Gill in profile driving his Volkswagen bus, I imagine his fingers being, in actuality, witching sticks for locating boulders. Gill, Ament, and I arrive at an amphitheater of rock where the ballet is to begin. John's dog, a red, half-Irish Setter named Gallo, scruffles up the backside of the amphitheater and races along the rim of the cliffs, then finds a pool of mud and water in which to play. Standing at the base of the Ripper Traverse, Gill breathes in gasps. He does not touch the rock, nor does he simply climb it. He in essence transcends the route. He is across it.

"Get The Hell Off That Rock"

Visiting the Needles in '75, John was ascending a one hundred-foot spire a short distance from the Needle's Eye parking lot on a humid, summer afternoon. In his words:

"I found myself pathetically grappling with slippery quartz crystals, patiently belayed by my wife, Dorothy. As I turned a corner halfway up the spire, two huge beer-drinking motorcyclists, clothed in what appeared to be uniforms of the Rumanian Iron Guard, spotted me. As they sat on the hood of the car of a petrified tourist, whose casual acquaintance they had just formed, they yelled to me, 'Get the hell off that rock!' With sweat pouring into my eyes and a dismal climbing performance jading my thoughts, I promptly shouted

back, 'Come get me!' A moment of tense silence gripped the Black Hills. Automobile traffic came to a halt, and touring families exchanged worried looks as they quickly rolled up their windows, locked their doors, and stuffed their small children into the back seats. The two motorcyclists focused their attention on me, with a look that was a perfect blend of cruelty and serendipitous pleasure. One of them effortlessly and with quiet arrogance pulled a beer can apart. The pieces tinkled to the ground. Remembering Dorothy on the ground, I quickly began mental calculations of distance and rappelling and running speed.

"Suddenly the two cyclists shook their heads, and their expressions changed to (of all things) bland indifference. They slid off the hood onto their Harleys and roared off with only the quickest glance at the daily and predictable casualty that unfailingly warmed the hearts of climbers: the Greyhound tour bus, as usual, had jammed against the rock and become stuck in the Needle's Eye tunnel, shedding its glassy tinsel to the satisfaction of children and climbers alike.

"My spirits bolstered by these fortuitous developments, I shouted around the corner of the spire to my belayer, 'It's OK Dorothy, they've gone,' only to hear her reply coming from a quarter mile away, 'That's good. I'll see you at the campground.'"

Fireside Chat

In January 1976, after a spaghetti dinner, Gill and I (Pat Ament) sat at the kitchen table of his house in Pueblo. We talked climbing for a couple hours, with a tape recorder running, then retired to the living room and continued the discussion until the recorder shut off. We noticed later that some of our comments seemed downright spaghetti-bloated. It was a "fireside chat" under the auspices of gathering information for a possible film. Gill's sense of humor, honesty, insight, and self-effacing perceptions were a kind of one-finger pull-up of humility. He was setting the standard in more ways than one.

The following are a few of his comments from that interview:

"I guess I've been very fortunate. The people that have bouldered with any degree of seriousness, with whom I have been acquainted, have all developed beautifully. I've always managed to pick something up from them, some little bit of technique, some form, style, things that are difficult to put your fingers on. It has always been an educational experience for me when I go out with a young climber who is quite good.

"I wouldn't say that I take a climber and mold him. These people, practically all of them, have an excellent reservoir of raw talent.

"I'm never quite sure what kind of day I'm going to have. Sometimes when I hit it, as the expression goes, I do extremely well. On other occasions, I've been known to do very poorly on just mediocre rock.

"I like bouldering sessions where you can afford to laugh at yourself and laugh at each other. I'll have to admit that, in some instances in the past eight or ten years, I have felt a bit like the classical, old, western gunfighter who is always being goaded into a shoot-out on Main Street.

"I'd rather go out with a friend, an acquaintance with whom I can relax a little, as opposed to someone to whom I must prove my absurdly impractical abilities all over again.

"My climbing philosophy has more or less stabilized at this point in life. I enjoy very competitive bouldering on occasion, not always. I get quite a bit of

satisfaction out of re-climbing routes that I have established. I've never felt compelled to do something that somebody else has done.

"From time to time I've been locked in the grips of a consuming passion for this route or that. But these have been periods of short duration. I don't hold a grudge against a nemesis. I've always enjoyed hiking. That's been an entirely separate activity for me within the mountain realm. When I go hiking, I usually don't even think about bouldering. I can walk beneath a beautiful boulder, and it will catch my eye just for a moment. I'd rather look at the flowers, the trees, and the birds.

"At the Hagermeister boulders, it must have been in the very early 1960's, I drove up for a session of bouldering, got out of the car, took my shoes and chalk, walked over to the standard slab route, and sat down. When I picked up my shoes to put them on, there was a twenty-dollar bill lying on the ground. So I put my street shoes back on, put the twenty-dollar bill in my pocket, took my shoes and chalk, went back to the car, and drove to town (Estes Park). And that was probably the most enjoyable bouldering session I've ever had.

"A good bouldering route is not one where the sequence of holds is perfectly obvious. It should be difficult to discover the correct sequence, and it should be difficult to execute the sequence. I do mathematical research, and you might be surprised by the very close parallel that exists between the two pursuits—one, apparently purely intellectual, the other apparently purely physical. In both instances, a person stands more or less at a frontier. It is enlightening to follow the proof of an established theorem, but far more satisfying to discover a new theorem. It is a creative enterprise, and I do not believe in painting a picture by numbers. One takes a blank canvas and does something original.

"In both bouldering and mathematics, you stand

upon the threshold of something new, something that requires not only brute force (whether it be physical or intellectual force) but a certain insight, a certain quantum jump from point to point. I don't mean making a physical jump, although sometimes that helps! Something is there that can be created, possibly, if one uses insight, intuition, etc., in order to make this quantum jump. One discovers that the bouldering route can be accomplished not by looking at each minute hold, foot by foot, but by looking at the overall route. One gets an instinctive feeling that it can be done and then starts looking closely for and at holds. You usually find that they are there."

Beartooth Range, Montana, 1976

"In bouldering, you're concerned as much—if not more—with form, style, elegance, and route difficulty as you are with getting to the top. There are all sorts of routes that don't end on the tops of boulders. Traverses,

for example. There are exceptional climbs that go part way up a cliff. You run into a blank wall, jump off, and that's the end of the bouldering problem. I've spoken with mountaineers about this sort of thing. It's usually difficult for them to adjust to a feeling for the small when they've been so concerned with the large. One little epigram that Chouinard once applied to bouldering was, 'Instant suffering.' I'll agree. It's as if you take a lengthy climb and squeeze it down into one or two moves. To compensate for decreased length, you increase the difficulty.

"Perhaps with an excellent mental attitude, you not only integrate your moves better but this in turn induces a telekinesis to levitate you slightly, even if it is only taking off a few ounces. A few ounces can make a tremendous difference.

"I feel that the bond of friendship, the roped team, may be a manufacturer as well as a transmitter of psychic energy."

Thoughts by Yvon Chouinard, in a taped conversation in Yosemite in the mid-'70s, seem to compliment Gill's thoughts:

"Climbing is still in a stage of pure physical movement, and the next step is going to be mind control. I think Gill has already gone into that, from watching him prepare for a boulder even in the late '50s. I would walk up to a boulder and just do it. He would sit below a route, do his little breathing exercises, and get his mind prepared, like a weight lifter walking up to a set of weights, getting his mind calmed down and his body ready to go. You're going to have to use meditation and Yoga to be able to get up some of the new climbs, because pure physical strength and technique are not going to be enough. You're going to have to climb as if you're two feet off the ground. I think it's going to be Zen and the art of rock climbing.

"That's what the book The Inner Game of Tennis is all about. They've taken people who are learning tennis, and one group goes out and

plays every day for two weeks while another group just sits down, meditates, thinks about improving, thinks about how they're going to swing the racket, getting it all set in their minds. The group that concentrates on it rather than plays becomes more skillful. Climbing is going to be the same way. You know, you can go out one day and play pool. And you're just an average player, but you simply look at the balls and know they're going to sink in the pockets. You grab the cue, you don't even think, then you run the whole table. You try to do it another day, and you can't. Why does that happen? When it gets to the point where we can, at will, conjure up these exceptional days, there'll be some incredible things occurring."

Advice On Training

I asked Gill in our "fireside" interview what advice he would give to climbers, with regard to training.

"I firmly believe that most people who wish to pursue bouldering can really benefit from formal gymnastics: rope climbing, still-rings, parallel bars, some high-bar, free exercise.... I have personally never used weights for training except to do a one-arm pull-up with twenty to thirty pounds in the other hand.

"What's worked best for me has been a combination of actual bouldering and certain forms of gymnastics. The weakest link between the climber and the rock is the fingers. Unfortunately, finger strength is probably the most difficult to develop and keep. It is the first to go with increased age. There are exercises that I have used to develop my fingers—fingertip chins on doorjambs and, ultimately, one-arm chins on the first joint of the fingers. This tends to develop power more than stamina. In most instances, a boulderer is concerned with a sudden burst of power, as opposed to long-term

stamina, but not always. The sort of strength one develops when working on the still rings seems to carry over to climbing. It gives you a certain amount of poise under stress, on overhangs for example. I was able to do butterfly mounts on the rings moderately easily and an iron cross. I did an inverted cross on occasion."

Gill, at Penny Ante Boulder, Pueblo

Gill said that to see good bouldering was to see a graceful display of athletic ability, the same type of precision apparent in good dance, the same balance, coordination, and strength. He added that bouldering was therapeutic.

February 1976, I (Pat Ament) visited the Hagermeister boulders, near Estes Park, with a young climber of prodigious talent and originality, David Breashears. A cold wind kept us from climbing, so we toured the rocks, and I pointed out Gill routes. I saw in David's eyes an energy and clarity. It seemed Gill's inspiration was to touch yet another generation.

As David Breashears later would say one day, "Gill is the true spiritual climber from whom we can all learn."

Master Of Rock

Using my conversation ("fireside chat") with Gill, I wrote a short book about him without his knowing. When the final draft of the book was finished, I mailed it to him. He told me that he was flattered. It was a "portrait," as I called it. In the book, I had invented a few phrases that Gill gratefully acknowledged—such as my referring to bouldering as "the poetry of mountaineering." At a small author-publisher celebration at my cabin in Eldorado Springs, the cork of a champagne bottle fired off and hit the ceiling when Gill's name was mentioned. Everyone took this to be a sign that the book would be a success. The book sold out quickly, a tribute to the respect climbers had for Gill.

Lost Canyon

May 1976, I bouldered with Gill on the buildings of the University of Southern Colorado. He did long, fingertip traverses, clamped a thick, square corner of concrete and ascended it. One route was a huge, aerial swing upward from a sloping finger-ledge. He also had routes inside the building that he did when the students were gone. He took me on a tour of the campus, and we wire-walked an occasional slack chain—a hobby we both enjoyed. The next day, Gill took me to Lost Canyon—a river-gully hidden in the prairie east of Pueblo and filled with large, angular blocks of Dakota sandstone. This was silent, cactus country, with a shallow river, Indian petroglyphs, and cottonwoods with leaves blowing. This was a typical Gill paradise. We returned on Thanksgiving to Lost Canyon. One of the most aesthetic routes was *the Juggernaut,* out and up the overhanging side of a large boulder. At one point, on finger holds, with his hands wide apart, and legs hanging free, he appeared to be in an iron cross on the rings.

On another occasion at Lost Canyon, I formulated a static variation of a dynamic route John had created on Penny Ante boulder. He was pleased with my solution, an application of difficult stemming techniques, using micro footholds, and he later reported to me that other of his friends who tried the problem could do the dynamic variation but not my static one. All of those climbers had stronger biceps than did I. It felt good now and then to find my own abilities, those that made me an individual. Yet my injured finger and shoulder, combined with a related loss of desire for training (not to mention my genetic disposition to put on the buxom pounds of my great grandmothers), prevented me from being an enduring competitor.

Gill's friendship with me, fortunately, was not contingent upon climbing prowess, and we amused ourselves on whatever difficulty matched the mood. He felt comfortable enough in our friendship to mock me relentlessly when his pre-teen daughter beat me (the English major) in a game of Scrabble.

Bears And Quiet Towers

Another afternoon in Pueblo, John and I traversed a man-made, stone wall above an open bear pit at the Municipal Zoo where my old gymnastic abilities seemed suddenly to come alive. They had not been forgotten altogether—as I began to imagine the consequences of a fall!

West of Pueblo, Gill found several six to eight hundred-foot granite buttresses on the side of a steep, wooded hillside. These "Quiet Towers," as he called them, appealed to him because they were broken by large ledges, or tiers, lending less of a sheer appearance and more of a tolerable one—exposure-wise. Here Gill could move from tier to tier up pinkish-white granite, enjoy the sky, and explore "the still faces of nature." In the mid-'70s, I followed him up one of these long, moderate solo climbs. At a section where I preferred to have a belay, he pulled a short, fifty-foot rope from his waist-pack and lowered an end of it to me. It appeared to be clothesline rope. When I asked if it was any good, he assured me, "Oh yes, I just bought it at K-Mart the other day."

New Blood

Gill formed good friendships with many outstanding boulderers, including Curt Shannon, Bob Murray, Lew Hoffman, Bob D'Antonio, Warren Banks, Chris Jones, and Bob Williams. Jim Holloway was an especially stunning bouldering talent whose company Gill esteemed.

"The fabulous Holloway," as Gill referred to him, reminisces:

"I had been climbing and bouldering for several years when Bob Williams invited me to go with him and John Gill in Pueblo. I was eighteen years old, and I was not going to miss this for anything. When we arrived at John's house, he showed us his set of rings in the backyard. After seeing front levers, handstands, etc., the kind of gymnastic moves you usually only see on television, I decided not to humiliate myself by attempting a two-arm hang, dead-man's swing, or such. I was going to save all the strength I had. We took John's car to the bouldering area. I even got to ride 'shotgun'—wow! Maybe Bob let me sit up front so that I would see the small, gold name-plate in the dashboard that said: This car made especially for John Gill (no joke). I was impressed.

"I learned a lot that day about dynamic moves, about doing them smoothly and in control. I was very interested in learning and in pushing my own limits. Now that I had seen this dynamic style done so flawlessly by John, I was hooked.

"Now—years later—having traveled to many of the areas across the U.S.A. that John bouldered at in the 1960's, I have learned more from his remarkable routes. Not only do they take great ability and

knowledge but also a certain awareness—all combined in a special way. I am grateful to have bouldered with John Gill. He has been the greatest inspiration in my bouldering, as I know he is to boulderers everywhere."

Jim Holloway

Curt Shannon on the Ripper Traverse

Bob Williams on *the Juggernaut*, Lost Canyon (Pueblo)

John Bachar and John Long visited Gill in the late 1970's. Here were two of the best California boulderers. Long had made a good show on the Fort Collins boulders and, with all his boisterous energy, weightlifter aggression, and linebacker impertinence, undoubtedly was an amusing study for Gill. Bachar himself found comedy in their visit and reported Long as having said, "O.K., Gill, let's do some B-2." Gill adds,

"I remember Long having a bit of a struggle his first visit, not making it up the Ripper, etc. But he was pleasant enough. I do recall catching John when he came

off of something on the Fatted Calf, and him being so surprised that I had that much strength—he was over two hundred pounds, I would guess. Dorothy got a kick out of him. She thought he was really cute!"

No matter how confident, energetic, muscular, opinionated, talented, competitive, or self-aggrandizing any certain climber might be, or how powerfully they ascended rock, Gill routes were, for the most part, owned by Gill and with more authority and beauty than by anyone else. Although Gill was quick to recognize other boulderers for their achievements, there could be no comparing oneself to Gill—he simply stood apart and remained the master, not only on rock but as a person in many ways.

1978 was marked by the death of John's father in Tuscaloosa, Alabama. John and Dorothy were in Seattle, on a trip, when John phoned his mother and learned the news. John's father had suffered from vascular problems.

In about 1979, my small, simple—yet clear—film of Gill, which I had named *The Silent Climber*, was honored with a financial award by the University of Geneva in Switzerland. Though crudely made, there was a magic to the film—at times Gill almost Charlie Chaplin-esque, and nothing for sound but my piano improvisations and a few words by Gill here or there. World famous bookseller Michael Chessler later would write that *The Silent Climber* was a masterpiece. I had lectured and would lecture widely with it, and never would I find an audience that was not completely excited and pleased with the film—despite its lack of production effects and its complete lack of typical sport-film sensationalism.

In the March-April, 1980, issue of *Climbing Magazine*, John Long wrote a piece about bouldering—showing a number of wide-angle photos of himself on boulders rather high above the ground. While Long admitted to Gill's inspiration, readers were made to wonder if at the same time Long was subtly denigrating Gill's well-expressed, almost "religious" philosophies and/or criticizing what writing had been done about Gill. In the article, Long wrote,

"A personal, sacred element is always experienced through the application of one's skill to a creative problem solving design. Yet the written exposure of this 'inner element' can so easily slip into trite hogwash, unveiling the shortcomings of both language and its designer. In fact, the excessive telecasting of one's inner climbing experiences is in poor taste and embarrassing—like forcing home-movies on a stranger. Anyway, a theological approach to bouldering proves to be just that much more psychological luggage to keep the mere contemplator grounded. The personal beauty of the sport is in the doing, and there alone."

This was an unusual statement coming from a graduate theology student (Claremont). In later years, Long would change his tune a bit and publish a long stream of personal "telecastings"—essays and books of climbing instruction that would be popular with the mainstream. The quaintest of these was an anthology he put together of "best writings," which included several of his own!

Self-belay, solo bouldering (top photo: *Little Overhang*, Bottom: *Black Streak*)

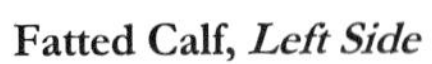
Fatted Calf, ***Left Side***

Fatted Calf Boulder, Gill on his most difficult route in Pueblo (static attempt), early 1980's

Traversing near *Ripper Traverse*, 1985

Difficult route in Little Owl Canyon

Difficult dynamic route, Little Owl Canyon (two photos)

He Didn't Care

In and around bouldering, Gill continued to find time for long solos that had "invigorating exposure." These involved no gear except for chalk and climbing shoes. By keeping levels of difficulty down, he was able to concentrate more on the pursuit of discovery in a classic mountaineering sense. Yet from moment to moment, a brief and real rock climbing challenge might appear. In an article in *The Climbing Art Magazine*, he wrote how one such solo on these high buttresses ended with an overhang and some climbing of a very exhilarating character. He wrote how he loitered on a face of rock above the overhang and played for a moment to convince himself that he "really could have done some alarmingly difficult climbing" had he wanted to.

Competition with his younger friends was a motivating factor in bouldering but played virtually no role in these longer, very private solo climbs. They fulfilled the simple ecstasy of being in the mountains and allowed him to move and flow and to enjoy climbing on his own terms, without the underlying sense of rules or expectations that often crept in during bouldering.

A very tall Scott Blunk spent part of the summer of 1979 bouldering with Gill and shares a few impressions of that time:

"It had been a great bouldering year for me: I did second ascents of some very hard routes at Horsetooth, climbed the Red Cross problems in the Tetons, and repeated most of the Gill routes in the Needles, including the Thimble via top-rope. That was all accomplished in the spring, so I was feeling mighty proud of myself by the time I moved down to Pueblo. I spent the summer there doing an internship at the State Hospital. I worked on a psychiatric ward, and it was a pretty crazy place—some people hallucinating about snakes, others lurking fearfully in corners, while still others nursed delusions of grandeur. I fit right into the latter category

with my firm belief that I was the best boulderer in the world.

"Of course I looked up Gill right away, and off we went. We toured the beautiful sandstone outcrops around Pueblo, each week visiting a new area. John put up with my youthful enthusiasm and impatience and, by way of example, taught me two important lessons about bouldering.

"He had one very powerful problem west of town where he hardly used his feet. He just cranked one-arms all the way up this bulging wall. I jumped on it immediately, thinking, 'Aha! Here's another coup for my war bag!' I failed miserably. Couldn't even do it using my feet. I went back to the hospital feeling lower than the imaginary snakes. And the worst thing about it was that Gill hadn't gloated over my failure at all. He just said that it was a neat route, one that he liked to do. That puzzled me, for I surely would have crowed over someone else's failure.

"The second lesson was just as puzzling. I had found an obscure little variant on the Penny Ante Boulder, something that I felt utterly compelled to do. After a lot of work, I succeeded. It turned out to be a long lunge on rather marginal holds. Gill tried it a couple of times without success, offered some praise for its difficulty, then apparently forgot about it. I was stunned. Here was a route in his home territory, and he didn't CARE?! I wondered if I should talk with a psychiatrist about this. Didn't you have to repeat a route just because it was hard?

"It took me awhile (years in fact) to figure out that bouldering is a very personal thing, that John climbed to satisfy his inner self rather than to satiate external expectations. Now that more than a decade has gone by, I can look back and smile at the struggles of an impetuous youth and, more importantly, remember a great summer's bouldering with John Gill."

Mystical States

Gill spoke of a mystical reality that, as he described, was "an extension of the hypnagogic state." He suggested that certain exertions in bouldering occasionally produced an apparent separation of "I-consciousness" and physical body, "similar to how the mind of a long-distance runner seems to soar above the automaton-like running form…."

The idea of the metaphysical in climbing would be the subject of bemused speculation, were it not advanced by Gill. Gill very obviously was not some kind of weird recluse with delusions, rather a respected mathematician and very much a realist. The credibility of his remarks could also be found in his ability as a climber. He seemed to describe these as mystical perceptions in part inspired by his interest in "the art of dreaming,"—described in Carlos Castenedas' fictional works on Don Juan. Gill felt that he had upon occasion slipped into an "alternate world." In utter solitude while ascending a steep tower in one of his climbing sanctuaries, he once had the ineffable experience of "merging with and re-emerging from the yellowish, polished surface of the granite." Experiences such as these were "entirely the consequences of meditative practices," for he never had used psychedelic drugs.

In contrast to such "removed," or "mystical," states, and moments of separation from climbing, Gill appreciated equally—if not more—the pleasure of "an intense realization OF the experience," the mind "saturated with kinesthetic awareness"—defined by grace, precision, and "momentum."

Just as sequences on gymnastics apparatus were combined with dynamics and by momentum, so could such values be added to the repertoire of the rock climber. In an essay on the subject of advanced dynamic climbing, Gill invited readers to "visualize a boulderer passing through two or more sequential moves," propelled upward by "the momentum from the first dynamic surge." Gill seemed fond of the phrase "kinesthetic awareness," meaning perhaps "self-realization," a turning inward where all realms—sensory, mental, athletic, artistic, intellectual, mystical, spiritual, and aesthetic—united.

Climbing had also, after all, to do with the aesthetic qualities of the mountains, with sensuous exploration, as much as it did with the exhilaration of ascending rock. In the way the rock had its varied look and feel and inspired its own type of clarity, so did nature stimulate the mental creativity of perception and charge the electrical energies of the mind.

Tachycardia

John saw a doctor after a brief experience with tachycardia and was informed that he should do more aerobic exercise. It was interesting that bouldering was insufficient to maintain cardiovascular conditioning. He followed the advice, walked more, hiked, kicked a soccer ball in a nearby park, and worked out on a Nordic track. But in fact abstaining from caffeine and cutting back on alcohol helped the most to clear up the problem.

Pueblo West And A Trip To England

John and Dorothy built a lovely but modest solar home in the prairie of Pueblo West in 1985. The location was pleasantly isolated and only a short drive to canyons to the west with granite where John could climb and explore.

John and Dorothy, Pueblo West

In March 1986, Gill gave a delightful, well-received talk, as a guest speaker at the biannual national conference of the British Mountaineering Council in Buxton, England. I was also a speaker and fortunate to be able to go with him and Dorothy to England. The British audience sat admiringly and listened to John's bouldering stories. They were amused by the philosophies that Gill presented in his humble, witty, but slightly verbose, academic style.

Pat Ament, John and Dorothy Gill, Buxton, England, 1986

At Guiseley Indoor Climbing Wall, in England, Gill demonstrated his abilities unexpectedly by casually approaching an overhang and doing a new route up it. The route involved an impressive aerial move. Witnesses to this short moment were dumbfounded, having not seen a person fly upward—while at the same time outward around the overhang—with such ease and using such small holds. Talk of the route spread instantly through England, although no one could remember exactly the holds or sequence Gill used. The story would seem to take on slightly exaggerated proportions in Jim Perrin's later description in *High Magazine*: "John reached up for a pinch-grip near the widest part of the wall's roof, pulled up dynamically and one-armed into a front lever, reached round the lip for a finger hold, swung free and pulled up, one-armed on his finger-tips, to the wall above...." I was one of the few who had witnessed the little ascent, and it struck me at the time as a somewhat typical Gill sequence.

In December of 1986, Gill was one of the guest speakers at the annual American Alpine Club meeting in Denver. In his talk, John put a statement by writer Somerset Maugham into the climbing vernacular: "There are three rules that will enable a climber to succeed at any pitch. Unfortunately, no one knows what they are." Gill also stated that he was "never one to be intimidated by the absence of danger."

That summer of '86, Patrick Edlinger, one of France's top competitive climbers, visited Boulder and asked me to show him the Gill test pieces at Fort Collins. After we visited Fort Collins, it seemed clear to me that Gill's bouldering throughout the 1970's had not been surpassed or even equaled as yet by the star climbers of the '80s.

"Failure" On Red Cross Rock

John returned in July of 1987, at the age of fifty, to the Tetons for an afternoon session with those old bouldering problems that were his first personal test pieces. His performance on the dynamic route on Red Cross Rock was disappointing. Reaching the small hold at the lip of Red Cross, he was fatigued and unable to continue over the top. He climbed several other routes, however, that he had established nearly thirty years earlier. Not many climbers had done the Red Cross route, although a few through the years had claimed success by an easier method created when a flake broke and left a comfortable fingertip hold. Gill knew the difference between that and the true problem. It also was a sad testament that a key feldspar crystal on his route *the Scab*, in the Needles, had been altered by someone (in 1980) and made more usable.

Chris Jones, a very strong, remarkable boulderer whose philosophies seemed to Gill to be especially compatible with his own, joined Gill in the Tetons on this return visit. At Red Cross Rock, after an energetic struggle, Chris succeeded at the difficult route—using the original Gill formula.

Chris Jones on the Mental Block, Fort Collins

Right Biceps Muscle Tears Loose From Elbow

Although Gill's experience went far beyond ordinary recreational rock climbing, recreation and play were rarely absent. He was equally drawn to very easy rock where he was able to move meditatively. Difficulty, it was apparent to his friends, played only a partial role in his love of climbing. Clearly the experience was a transcendent one, whether engaged in the challenge of an almost impossible overhang or scrambling up an long, easy slant of rock.

Part of that transcendence has been the lighthearted spirit that is one of Gill's qualities. He is acutely observant, wise, and possesses a fine inner being. Admitting to his own particular quirks and specialization, he never fails to credit friends with every inch of height that they earn, his generosity as spectacular as his climbing moves.

In October of 1987, at the age of fifty, Gill was bouldering in surprisingly good form. He was heartened to experience a physical renewal. He could still do front levers and one-arm, fingertip pull-ups. Yet he also admitted that taking his golden retriever Dusty for a stroll across the quiet prairie, dining out with friends, or writing about climbing instead of doing it were becoming increasingly attractive. Yet there were the youthful "surges of enthusiasm."

In an attempt to make his tenth or so ascent of the *Micro-Shield*, a short, severe problem at that time unrepeated by others, on granite near his home in Pueblo, his foot slipped from a 2mm hold. As his weight came suddenly onto his extended right arm, the biceps muscle was torn from the forearm bone. Aside from the pain, there was the gruesome effect of the muscle more or less "rolling" up to his shoulder under the skin of his arm. The surgeon who successfully re-attached the muscle speculated that the muscle had probably been held in place by little more than scar tissue—a testament to years of dynamic moves. The other arm very well could go in the same manner—if Gill was not careful.

Gill on the *Micro-Shield*, Pueblo

After months of recovery and with a great deal of effort (he designed his own therapy), John was able to begin a few moderate exercises. He decided, however, that he would never attempt aerobatics, or dynamic climbing, again.

Return To *Delicate Arete*

Any number of climbers visited Pueblo and reported that Gill was a formidable climber even with the new preventive care that he applied to each route. A year and a half after his injury, he could again do a one-arm pull-up with his injured (right) arm.

Except for a periodic return to the boulders "to assess the damage," Gill's climbing more and more returned to its origins—found in long, usually moderate solo ascents in solitude, the way he had found adventure as a young man. His passion for extreme bouldering was disappearing. There was no desire to repeat the experience of a detached muscle, or otherwise destroy himself, in one explosive dynamic move. Excellent solace and considerable challenge were to be found in these longer, exploratory solos.

He returned again to the Tetons in July of '89, to his old haunt of soaring, gray peaks where there were lakes and where he could encounter "a veritable jungle of large, leafy green plants rioting among huge Douglas-fir and ponderosa pine." Clouds circled the mountains and sent shadows across meadows of lupine. Rock rose into clear Wyoming air. Carrying only a couple slings and a fifty-foot length of nylon rope purchased at K-Mart, he began up *Delicate Arete*—the ridge he had made the first ascent of in 1958. He still remembered vividly his second ascent of the route, where he had found himself on a barren edge of rock on tiny holds while buffeted by strong winds—"so close to peeling," as he wrote in *the Climbing Art Magazine*, "that reality itself lost its cohesion."

In the following article, he describes his return in 1989 to *Delicate Arete*:

"I have had tense moments in former years, clinging like an ant while unpredictable, angry winds pulled and pushed—an eternity of several minutes. Is it possible that I did, in fact, slip from those minute

footholds? Has all that has happened in the presumable intervening years been illusion, woven with blinding speed into my last corporeal moments? Am I destined to return now, slip through a fold in time and greet the angry slabs as they rush toward me?

"The body is cold, it wants action, so I set aside these curious reflections and get on with the dance. Thirty years experience should be safeguard enough....

"The first few raindrops land on the already slick, high-angle slabs, and my apprehension returns....

"I am at the base of the corner of the yellow wall.... All I see is steep rock, a few small cracks, and unnerving exposure.... I climb rapidly for thirty feet or so and pause. Then in a brief moment of middle-aged abandonment, I follow a whim and step around the corner onto the yellow wall.

"I am instantly appalled by my ill-conceived action. This is no good—really difficult, practically vertical terrain, terribly exposed. The smooth, yellow pegmatite is inches from my face, its tiny crystals shimmering with moisture. Barely breathing, I move to the right with infinite caution—foot, then hand, foot, and then hand. Finally I am secure once again on the easy corner, and I relax and contemplate this egregious lapse. I have always felt that spontaneity is essential in finding a path upon the rock that makes the spirit soar, but this brief experience points to the danger of a more capricious, almost senile behavior."

Life Savers

In the fall of '89, Gill found a bit of moderate, solitary climbing on the limestone cliffs of the Calanques, in southern France, while he attended a mathematics meeting at the French government's International Center for Mathematical Research on the Luminy Campus of the University of Marseilles. By following a short path from his lodging (a huge, pink converted convent on the wooded campus), he encountered the blue Mediterranean spread out beautifully and splashing gently at the base of white, limestone cliffs.

In 1990, at age fifty-three, Gill returned again to the Tetons and with a "playful attitude" soloed a seven hundred-foot new climb up the east side of the south face of Satisfaction Buttress. As Life Savers dissolved in his mouth, he ascended at his own speed, losing himself in exploration, with an occasional moment of excitement or challenge. At the finish of the climb, he experienced a fulfillment that was "mildly religious." In his usual understatement, he wrote in an article that his personal metaphor for this sort of climbing was "making a mountain out of a molehill."

On other "scrambles" during this trip to the Tetons, he continued to find excitement—for example descending off one route, where he was forced to climb through a short waterfall on "slick, overhanging rock."

Gill gave the type of soloing he particularly enjoyed on higher rocks the name "menu climbing," then refined that to "option-soloing"—whereas many potential lines exist, with frequent easy scrambling alternatives, and many branch points to allow for spontaneous decisions.

August of 1991, on another visit to the Tetons, an intended option-solo materialized into the more serious feel of "free-soloing." He found himself on smooth, water-polished granite, making a few "airy steps" high up on the third tier of Trinity Buttress. One can assume that it was Gill's tremendous skill that made the consequences of these events manageable.

In a present tense memoir, he writes of this ascent:

"I move across a boulder field and up a steep, grassy slope to a tiny cave hidden in the trees at the base of Trinity Buttress—a tiered cliff. After stowing my blue daypack, I put on my climbing shoes, belt pack, and

coiled rappel line, and move up around the left corner of the cave onto an exposed but undistinguished ridge. I scan the buttress above. My route will be devious—three large cliffs are separated in a complex fashion by huge ledges covered with trees and brush.

"The transition from scrambling to climbing, that moment when you first glance down and see rocks and grass far beneath the contours of your feet, induces a heightened perception and a subtle change in body chemistry. I feel more locked into the evolving matrix of the present and less prone to drift in time and place. I move up the arete, ascending several minor steps in an increasingly airy environment, frictioning over rounded corners. Easy terrain on my right—I could scramble, practically walk up there if I wish—steep cliffs on my left, long and exposed. That's where previous climbs have been made.

"I move into a thirty-foot dihedral with abundant holds and climb quickly upward, passing in astonishment what appears to be a fresh Charlet-Moser piton: is this to be a dream-like day in the twilight zone of a thirty-year distant past? Whatever the context, this is the first fun pitch of the day—no grass, dirt or shrubs, just clean, firm rock. Above, I enter a strange, chaotic realm of precipitous rock walls, steep grassy ledges, and towering evergreens, some leaning over the corners of vast overhangs, their roots groping blindly into space. Color is everywhere—in the texture of the rock and the brilliant green of the trees.

"I move up through this turbulent landscape, guided more by whimsy than strategy. I imagine myself in an ancient poem—a medieval fairy tale—as I scramble along vertiginous ledges and over short bulges of lichen-covered granite, across precariously steep dirt slopes on the very edge of concave palisades, until finally reaching a broad shelf guarded by stately firs, the sentries of time.

Beautiful white and tan slabs of polished granite sweep upward from here, two hundred feet to the top of the second tier of cliffs, capped by an uneven but continuous overhang. I pause for a few moments, thinking that at the age of fifty-four my climbing career has come full circle. I have returned to the origins of spirit, found in the simplicity of my earliest and most naive ascents.

"With some apprehension, I scan the long line of the overhang above me until spotting an obvious break where exposed scrambling may carry me through. Tiptoeing now, up and across to the west on lovely, firm, and slightly sculptured rock, an occasional optional move of unnecessary difficulty to add spice to my adventure, and I am suddenly near the crest of the overhang. I sense the tingle of exposure as I move up an easy crack to a foot-wide ledge directly beneath an abrupt, ten-foot step. If I negotiate a couple of elementary moves now, with my hands above on slabby holds, I'll be up and through the barrier.

"As I balance on my exposed perch, I hear voices of a climbing party across the couloir on the southwest ridge of Storm Point—a half mile away. A female climber, assertive to the point of belligerence, is leading two good-natured men up a series of granite slabs. Her instructions ring clearly through the canyon. Instinctively, I begin to move in the direction she indicates! I knew long ago that the tough, hard-man, thoroughly masculine image of climbing would eventually vanish. I didn't foresee the peculiar androgynous analogue that would evolve, however.

"My attention interrupted by this display, I step over the bulge—exaggerating a simple move in the process. A trivial distraction, yet my technique has been degraded. I move quickly up onto dirt and scree slopes leading to a large boulder sitting a few feet from the vertical immensity of white and yellowish granite that

forms the last, most significant part of Trinity Buttress.

"It's not good that I lost my concentration for a moment on the pitch below. That's not the way to endure in this solitary and dangerous meditation, this slowly deliberate, vertical stroll on edges of hard granite reality. In soloing, the margins of safety are maximized by shutting out anything other than the immediate technical requirements of climbing.

"Time for a few Life Savers. After some deliberation, I decide to climb on the eastern part of the buttress wall on rock that rises to a prominent shelf two hundred feet up. To the west, the rock is vertical and has few if any comfortable resting places. From my philosophical perspective, it lacks the virtue of available relaxing sections where a middle-aged explorer can recharge. I move upward and to the left, following a diagonal seam toward a small, rectangular block perched high on a minor ridge. The face I ascend becomes vertical toward the end of the pitch, capped by a slight overhang, but the holds are large and climbing easy. I fully expect to find a simple way up the last twenty feet above the block to the shelf seen from below. But when I arrive at the block I am face to face with uniformly steep, smooth, yellowish rock of severe appearance and considerable exposure—far too risky for unroped exploration.

"To the right of the crest, however, I see a favorable pattern of holds. Amazing how one's perspective changes. A few seconds ago, while beneath this section, I dismissed the possibility of going straight up, due to the exposure and wickedly smooth nature of the rock. Now I see that a couple of elementary but airy moves on newly discovered ledges will take me up the remainder of the face.

"Several minutes of increasingly disciplined, tentative steps off the block, onto the rock above, then back onto the block bring me to the point where

determination exceeds the sense of jeopardy, and I move up a steep dihedral for several feet. I step around a corner, stretching my right leg to reach a ledge that slopes away from me and down and is carved into the wall above a small overhang far above the trees. I would never attempt this elementary but unprotected move without the new technology of sticky rubber soles.

"A short scramble leads to the shelf. Without pause for rational planning—deplorable but typical behavior when I get wound up in this frenetic sport—I start up a high-angle crack that appears to terminate thirty feet above at a ten-foot vertical face. The face seems replete, from its rough facade, with abundant edges. It should provide an easy exit into dirt gullies above that are filled with scree and bordered by shrubs and trees. The climbing on the smooth stone quickly becomes a little harder, and I run out of comfortable, horizontal holds. I move continuously, stemming and cross-pressuring my way up an inside corner until I reach the small face. At last some sloping footholds and a good hold for one hand...a chance to secure and pause and suppress the niggling anxieties that threaten to disturb the smooth flow of climbing technique.

"Slightly out of balance and with considerable space beneath my toes, I can see no more holds above me. Feeling that I am at the end of my hypothetical rope, I search for a way to negotiate a few feet of intimidating rock without calling on bouldering skills that I have largely avoided using since my injury.

"I still my mind and press tiny sparks of apprehension into the subconscious and calm the viscera, and I am ready to receive instructions. And... yes... my body drifts a step to the right, above the emptiness, and I am now nearly below a ledge, and I find a handhold and a sloping foothold and step up and stand above this thing I have become part of.

"It is over, and I scramble the remaining few feet to the top. I lose the descent path on the bottom tier of cliffs and wander back and forth across the wilderness of overhanging walls and tree-covered shelves. I follow ledges that lead nowhere. I traverse steep, dangerous, earthen slopes, rappelling three times, until I am down to the level of the cave and my blue pack. It is 4:30, and I am weary and hungry. This day has been a bit more than I expected. The difficulties were, I am certain, less than they seemed, but the continual probing of the unknown strains the eye and the nerve and leaves the mind unsettled, insecure in the subtle turbulence of an existential ripple."

Lew Hoffman met Gill on this trip to the Tetons and, in the following account, captures a little of the spirit of his friendship with Gill:

"John and I had occasionally talked of coordinating summer Teton visits. August of '91 finally found us at Gros Ventre campground with hopeful agendas and a dubious weather pattern. After I returned from a mostly rainy, two-day alpine effort, I cooked a pre-arranged clam sauce spaghetti dinner and waited for John at the campground.

"He drove up as the next wave of rain soaked Jackson Hole. We hunkered under my meager tarp and dined as John recounted his day's adventure—he'd hiked into the Tetons, bushwhacked up to a face he'd been considering for a few decades, free-soloed the route (unlisted in any guide) up and down, and beat the storm back to the valley floor.

"At the Jenny Lake ranger cabin that August, the common, repeated wisdom was that alpine activity, especially new routes, had dropped sharply since the action was on the new 'sport' crags south of Jackson and on recently bolted Blacktail Butte (lines Gill had free-soloed thirty years before). I guess sport is where and how one finds it.

"Occasionally I hear a good, apocryphal Gill story and relay the story to John who is always amused and ready with an honest denial or truthful retelling. Here are two mini-myths. In Colorado Springs, after

inelegantly scratching my way up a Garden of the Gods problem (a mighty step upward to the first foothold, followed by a crux pull upward off of smoothly-weathered tourist initials chiseled long ago into the boulder), a local climber informed me that John Gill had done the problem first try, using only his left arm. John later said he'd never bouldered in the Garden.

'During a foray to the Black Hills in the late '70s, stories were told around a campfire. Pete Cleveland's tales of extra-curriculars at the "sex cave" were great, but I didn't nasal snort a swallow of beer until the inevitable Gill story. Not even rock-related, this one had a group of climbers relaxing in a Custer bar when John joined them. John demonstrated a balance training routine, presumably before quaffing too many brews, by tiptoeing across empty beer bottles arranged along the bar top!

'While on a sandstone bouldering outing in the mid-'80s, John mentioned his rekindled interest in granite—Black Hills-style—bouldering he'd found in the mountains west of Pueblo. Gill envisioned climbing a vertical, totally blank slab. On a fall day about a month later, we visited a granite area. John led me on a circuit of Needles-quality boulders. At the circuit's end, John and I spied and started 'one last new route,' while his wife Dorothy broke out our picnic lunch. We'd nubbined up to a blank spot, which we now protected with a top-rope. After a few personal dynamic efforts to span the blank (all of which ended with my swinging horizontally on the rope at John's eye level), he glided the gap statically with a surprising reach involving a step on a micro-edge and a two-fingered pull into a one-arm mantel. I call the route the Stretcher, and I suppose no one has tried this hidden classic since.

'Flashing the route left John elated and Dorothy and I impressed. After John downclimbed the backside of the boulder, Dorothy said he'd appeared to use a magical rubber arm to effect the stretch. John laughed and attributed the feat to the 'mystical element' of climbing."

Gill soloed a couple of long routes near Estes Park, Colorado, this same summer. He found a "moderate" route up the six hundred-foot Sundance Buttress and later, with his good friend Chris Jones, a master boulderer, soloed a rock buttress of Twin Sisters.

The Experience Is Everything

In the following treatise, Chris Jones reflects about Gill and describes a climb near Pueblo that Gill and he soloed together:

"'Now, around this corner there is more exposure. It gives me a different feeling.' I looked across to the corner, and the several hundred feet of exposure below it, and thought to myself, 'Hmm... yes, John, I can believe that it does.' No doubt John was going to be feeling a heightened sense of elation when soloing this next section. No doubt this next section was going to give me a different feeling as well—heightened fear most likely.

"John and I were unroped about half-way up one of his favorite soloing rocks, a two-tiered, 600-foot buttress in the mountains west of Pueblo. Despite my apprehension, I was glad to be here with John and that he was sharing this experience with me.

"Actually, he was sharing more than the experience of simply climbing a route without a rope. John has found for himself, and was teaching me, a novel variant of the unroped game. I will attempt to recount the lesson.

"The idea is not simply to ascend, but to have the freedom to ascend in precisely the way that feels right at the moment. The selection of what is to be climbed is very important. A long crack in smooth granite would not be appropriate, since it would be too constraining. Best is a fairly broad face, generally of lower angle and with plenty of holds, featured with a steeper step here, a smoother slab there, and the occasional ledge and overhang. There must be plenty of choices as to where to go, what feature to ascend. One must be free to choose a more difficult way than the easiest, if that is what strikes the fancy of the moment. The rock must be a menu, for this 'menu-soloing.' The choices, freedom, movement, mental acuity inspired by the exposure, warmth of the sun, feel of the rock – the EXPERIENCE *is everything.*

"For me to practice menu-soloing properly, I needed milder selections than what this rock was immediately presenting. Looking across to the exposed corner, I decided I'd be ascending the easiest way I could find and would console myself by clinging with approximately twice the force

that was actually needed to keep me attached. Not so for John. He climbed lightly and quickly, with complete confidence. He was always way up ahead of me, either happily entertaining himself with his selections or patiently waiting for me as I slowly and carefully made my way to his position. I think he could have climbed this thing four times in the time it took me.

"John pointed out some of the items he had found satisfying in the past. He showed me a slab that one time had exactly fit his appetite, which he thought was perhaps 5.9. It was just to my left, ten feet out from the relatively comfortable dihedral I was in, with 500 feet of exposure. Since it appeared to have no holds, it certainly looked at least 5.9. If I went there, I knew I'd be biting off more than I could chew.

"To know John is to know that he climbed that slab precisely because it WAS what suited his appetite at the time. Whether I or anyone else ever knew that he had climbed it was entirely an aside. Social goals, the desire for this or that accomplishment, this or that gain in the hierarchy among one's peers—all of that, I think, has receded for John as he has focused intensely on pure internal experience.

"John penned an essay in 1979, 'Bouldering: A Mystical Art Form,' in which he wrote of 'internal' aspects of bouldering and rock climbing in contrast to social, or 'outer,' aspects. One thing particularly impressive about John's bouldering is that he took difficulty so far, when in his case it has been generated so largely by internal motivation. I wouldn't say his motivation has always been ENTIRELY internal—he is human after all—but the level of difficulty that a boulderer is able to enjoy without regard to social reward seems one good measure of ability.

"In the fall of 1987, my wife, Alicia, and I were watching John as he balanced delicately in a tenuous position on a nearly holdless, gently overhanging face in the hills west of Pueblo. His toes were edging on tiny flakes, and his fingers were pulling on equally tiny flakes. After gathering a certain stability, his right arm shot to a high hold. On this route, which John had climbed some years earlier and had repeated several times, there is an almost irresistible tendency for the left hand and both feet to lose their place once the high hold is caught. Still strong enough, at age 50, to hold onto the high hold with his right arm in a one-arm pull, John held on after his feet and left hand came away from their micro-flakes.

"Then he quickly dropped back to the ground. 'Well, I've pulled

my bicep.' He said it so matter-of-factly that I figured what he meant was that he tore some muscle tissue—which sounded bad enough. But in fact the tendon attachment at his elbow had pulled entirely away, and he knew it immediately. It was a very painful injury, surely the kind to end a bouldering career at his age, yet he did not complain. He simply held the arm immobile, even maintained a relatively cheerful disposition, as we drove to the emergency room.

'Hopefully John won't mind too much if I bring a device from the 'outer' world of climbing—difficulty ratings—into what I want to say now. The route on which he injured himself has only been climbed by one other boulderer (Curt Shannon). I was not able to climb it myself. I think it must be about V7—in the modern bouldering rating system—and an unusually technical one. In his last years of severe dynamic bouldering, John worked on another route in the same granite area—a route that is certainly at least V9. His best attempt was better than what anyone else has been able to do on the route. I have no doubt that John would eventually have climbed this V9 had he not been injured. And I suspect that it would have been all the same to him whether or not anyone ever knew he was still able to climb something so difficult. No one else I know would work on a route this difficult without being driven, at least in part, by a powerful social current.

'On the Fatted Calf boulder, west of Pueblo, there is an overhanging groove, on which John was able to pull laterally, do a technical dynamic spring to a hold over the lip, hang on with one hand, and pull over the top (mid-1970's). This route is also about V9. Jim Holloway is the only other boulderer who has climbed it.

'John didn't mind telling me that this was a route that he did spend a number of days learning before the ascent. When I asked him how many days this was, his reply was 'maybe 5 or 6.' Of course, 5 or 6 days are far fewer than used on the most difficult routes (Jim Holloway spent as many as thirty days working his masterpiece V11's). Without any real competition in the 1960's, and plenty of virgin bouldering to be done, it was very rare for John to spend more than one to three days working a route. This is the reason that John did not create a great many V8's and V9's, and tended to work in the V5 to V7 range primarily. Few boulderers or sport climbers today, with training methods and rock gyms,

can match how quickly John, with his dedication to training, was able to climb most of his routes. For example, John climbed all three of the main routes on the Mental Block west of Fort Collins—the Left, Center, and Right (Pinch Overhang)—in a single day in late 1968.

"Then there were the 'routines' (as opposed to 'routes') that John did, where he would make use of his shoulder-arm-finger power—a power that still is not possessed by any of today's top boulderers and sport climbers. For example, just to the left of the V9 route on the Fatted Calf is a route on which, after reaching a high, sloping, fingertip hold with his right hand, his left hand still down low, John would make a point to not put his feet back on the rock. From this hang he would do a slow one-arm pull-up on the sloping fingertip hold until his left hand was over the lip, on which he could do another one-arm pull-up before manteling. Even today, in this age of sport climbing, there are no standards by which to apply a rating to such a routine.

"With the strength to do up to three full one-arm pull-ups on a five-eighths-inch, flat surface with his wrist forward, it is amazing that John also acquired the fine technique that allowed him to climb all the delicate, technical problems that he has. In the years since boulderers and rock climbers first became aware of the strength to which John trained himself, there have been just a few who have trained their strength to something near his. Each can attest that it is very difficult to acquire the best footwork when strength alone allows one to solve so many problems. Yet there was John: delicately poised on those tiny flakes just prior to the move which pulled his biceps muscle.

"A year after the surgery to re-attach his tendon, John was able to do a one-arm pull-up with either arm once again. Not wishing to risk another serious injury from dynamic bouldering, however, he has focused on his particularly internal form of soloing. I see him now, on the rock far above me, a solitary figure, a free and inventive mind engaged in pure experience."

In an essay published in *the Climbing Art Magazine* of fall 1991, Gill encouraged other middle-aged climbers to try option soloing. The essay's first paragraph:

"Each year the approach of summer rejuvenates me. Academic activities and their attendant social vexations are swept by a cleansing mental tide, and I contemplate the rhapsodic days of solitary climbing that lie ahead. In the best spirit of play I remove myself from undertakings that have purpose, and focus on one that has only meaning."

It has meant a great deal to Gill to be able to view the vast expanse of prairie around his home, to see blue sky, or distant peaks with snow, and see the horizon in any direction. He has come to appreciate the prairie itself, hawks, coyotes, the fragrance of sage and brown earth.... A given evening, moonlight brightens the prairie, the sky almost as bright as day.

Dorothy

While director of personnel working full time at Parkview Episcopal Hospital, Dorothy finished her bachelor's degree in business by attending Regis College in Colorado Springs. Gill observed to me (Pat Ament) about Dorothy:

"She has an amazing amount of energy, commitment, and perseverance. She's thinking now of getting a master's degree. I'm extremely proud of the way things have developed for her, what she's done with her professional life. Alongside her busy career, she has managed to raise her children and my child—for Pam was staying with us full time during one period. Dorothy was never a climber—she knew nothing about climbing when I met her. I took Dorothy, her children, and Pam out to a local area and showed them what rock climbing was all about, put them on a rope, and we had a reasonably good time, but Dorothy had no interest in rock climbing. I have never put pressure on anyone to learn to climb."

John spoke of Dorothy's accomplishments, how Parkview Hospital is a leader in translating Dr. Edward Deming's philosophy to health care and how Dorothy has been to meetings with quality gurus at GM and Ford and spoken with Dr. Deming.

She was born in Budapest in August of 1938, her father a prominent architect, designer, and member of parliament. Dorothy, her two older sisters, and her mother and father were evacuated just before the end of World War II and resettled in the small Bavarian village of Neureichenau, near the Czechoslovakian and Austrian borders. While there, she lived a Heidi-like life—complete with wooden shoes—for five years. In 1950, her family found a sponsor in Billings, Montana, and Dorothy lived there until she left for college. Dorothy's father, Eugene Padanyi-Gulyas, a fascinating and highly intelligent gentleman, lived under a Soviet death threat for many years as a result of participating in Admiral Horthy's Government.

Eugene showed an avid interest in mathematics, and both he and John were fond of the writings of Tielhard de Chardin. Gill had several long conversations with Eugene on philosophical matters before Eugene died in 1980. John's own father died in 1978.

John and Dorothy journeyed to Neureichenau in August of 1990 and spent several days in a lodge overlooking a community swimming lake. They hiked and visited places Dorothy remembered, including the large farmhouse where she and her family occupied one room, a very sentimental time for Dorothy. They then drove to Hungary and explored the country while John participated in an international conference on approximation theory at Kecskemet.

Dorothy wasted no time in becoming a vice president at Parkview Episcopal Hospital—quite a progression from entry-level bookkeeper.

Award For Excellence

John, a full professor since 1980, was awarded the 1991 Provost's Award for Excellence in Scholarship by the University of Southern Colorado. His career as a mathematician was impressive. He had served for a couple years, in the early '80s, as department chair at the University. He was active in the Mathematics Association of America (MAA), serving as chair of the Rocky Mountain Section in the early '80s while also on the Board of Governors of the MAA. He was twice president of the University of Southern Colorado Sigma Xi Chapter. His general area of math is complex function theory. He began his research with a publication in the *Transactions* of the American Math Society, concerning infinite compositions of linear fractional transformations. Over the next twenty-five years, he wrote many papers, appearing in publications such as: *Proceedings of the AMS, Mathematica Scandinavia, Proceedings of the Norwegian Royal Society of Arts & Science, Journal of Computational & Applied Math, Journal of Applied Numerical Mathematics, Bulletin of the Calcutta Math Society, Springer-Verlag Lecture Notes in Math, Rocky Mountain Journal of Mathematics,* and others.

Along the way, John introduced an effective and geometrically inspired method of accelerating the convergence of continued fractions. He blended aspects of complex dynamics with the convergence theory of analytic continued fractions; extended the principle of limit periodic behavior beyond continued fractions; generalized a classical theorem on contraction mappings; and discovered an efficient method of computing fixed points of functions defined by series, continued fractions or products. He introduced complex dynamics of inner and outer composition structures, as well.

John has been active in a small but international group of mathematicians interested in the analytic theory of continued fractions and related topics. In 1991, he started a limited-subscription specialty research journal, *Communications in the Analytic Theory of Continued Fractions.*

John chalking up

The journal, with John as managing editor, would be particularly helpful to mathematicians from behind the former iron curtain—by publishing several papers of theirs.

John's teaching assignments were mostly at the undergraduate level, since USC is basically an undergraduate institution, although when they sporadically offered a master's degree Gill taught graduate analysis classes. In 1992, he received the Outstanding Faculty Award for the School of Science & Mathematics at USC. It was his feeling that he was achieving a good balance between climbing and academic-professional activities. A number of excellent mathematicians were also excellent climbers: Leigh Ortenberger, who wrote the definitive Teton Guide, Dave Rearick, John Stannard (math and physics), Helmut Rohrl, Bill Buckingham, Bill Briggs, R.F. Williams, etc. John says,

"There is an affinity between math and climbing. It has to do with independence of effort and good pattern recognition skills, coupled with a desire to solve problems and explore."

Grampa Gumby

Pam Gill, living in New York City, found a profession in real estate management, then moved on to the Fund Raising Department of the Brooklyn Center for Performing Arts

John's daughter Pam with his mother Bernice, 1992

Dorothy's daughter, Susanne, bought her Godparents' home in Pueblo where she lived with Dylan, not far from John and Dorothy. Chris, Dorothy's son, living in the Bay Area, became father to a daughter, Nicole Rose—whom, according to Dorothy, "is as feminine as Dylan is all boy." Chris and his wife Marci would in time move to Denver. John and Dorothy have loved being grandparents and living close enough to spend time with Dylan. In return, Dylan conferred upon the distinguished John Gill the name "Gumby" (later changed to the more prosaic "Grandpa").

Dylan, John, and Collette, Pueblo

Curt Shannon likens grandpa Gumby to "a normal guy":

"He could be the guy standing next to you in line at the supermarket. Your odds of this are greatly enhanced if you buy your

groceries in Pueblo. Although he is one of the few genuine legends in the world of climbing, establishing the benchmarks by which generations of boulderers will be measured, a remarkable thing about John Gill is how unremarkable he at first appears. When at home, and not working on his new mathematical journal, he can often be found reading, playing catch with the dog, or participating in likewise non-legendary stuff. At his home one evening prior to a post-bouldering-session dinner, for example, his grandson, Dylan, was racing around the concrete with a fire truck—obviously en route to at least a five-alarm blaze. Gill was in hot pursuit of Dylan in order to save the catfish—which in this instant were certainly an endangered species, balanced as they were on top of the grill. Every time I see Dylan over at John's house, I try not to think about being out-bouldered by somebody's grandfather.

"Most people have had the opportunity to watch Olympic caliber gymnastics, if not in person then at least via broadcast into their living room. At this level of the sport, the gymnast is required to perform maneuvers which approach the limits of what is humanly possible while at the same time making them look effortless and almost trivial. 'Why, I bet I could do that,' sometimes occurs to a misled viewer if the gymnast has been particularly flawless in his execution. On my first visit to Little Owl Canyon with Gill, substitute Gill for the gymnast (me for the viewer). You should, by now, have a fairly good idea what happened. I came away disappointed yet inspired, having succeeded at very little, in spite of the fact that nothing Gill showed me that day looked very hard.

"That experience had a tremendous impact on my development as a boulderer, as have all of my subsequent outings with Gill. After finally making it across the Ripper Traverse, in a style that did a great disservice to one of his masterpieces, I remember Gill commenting that my technique was 'effective.' He can always put a positive twist on my sometimes less than stellar efforts.

"I was attempting the second ascent of the problem that ended Gill's dynamic bouldering, and John was there taking photos. The Micro-Shield problem, as it's called, involves a very difficult dynamic move from an iron-cross position on razor blade holds to what is essentially the summit. All kinds of thoughts were going through my head. How bad do I want this problem? This move detached Gill's biceps muscle. Not that my

biceps are anything to brag about, but I am figuratively and still quite literally attached to them and want it to stay that way. After completing the route and scrambling down the rock's backside, John commented, 'Well somebody had to do it, and it may as well have been you.'"

Repeats Of The Thimble

In 1991, *Climbing Magazine* reported that John Sherman had made the second solo ascent of Gill's Thimble route in the Needles. Sherman was somewhat embarrassed by this account, for he did not claim to have made the second ascent. This was the magazine's claim. The history of the Thimble subsequent to Gill's remarkable ascent was, in fact, uncertain, borne of stories. It was said that the route had been done by Pete DeLannoy, and by an eastern climber, or by "some southern kid," possibly by Eric Zschiesche (sp?) from North Carolina, after top-roping, and possibly by Kris Kline (also from North Carolina), or by Keith Pike, or by Brent Kertzman.... Pete DeLannoy did in fact solo some version of the route in August of 1987. Seven years earlier, he had tried the route on top-rope as a beginner in the company of Kevin Bein but failed at it. During those seven years, he trained and bouldered a lot. One day in the Needles, not thinking he would solo the route, he saw it and felt the inspiration to try it. He succeeded. So much time had passed between this ascent and his top-rope attempt as a neophyte, that it could hardly be classified as a "rehearsed ascent." DeLannoy remembers getting to the top and feeling proud but wishing that the ascent had not been tainted by his previous top-rope attempt of the route—even if long ago.

A day after this ascent, DeLannoy was astonished to watch "a climber from North Carolina" climb it solo twice. The climber received no advice from DeLannoy and apparently had not tried the route before. This person was, according to DeLannoy, "a character who had long arms and had a cat on a leash." Khris Kline later phoned me (Pat Ament) to say that he indeed was the person with the cat on the leash. DeLannoy recalls how, on Khris's second time up the route, he was shaking so bad that it seemed he was going to hit the pavement. When told of this ascent, Gill said with a chuckle, "I'm glad someone did it who was from the South."

A rumor that a 1984 solo of the route had been made by Brent Kertzman was something at least a couple of local Needles climbers doubted, since "such an ascent did not seem in keeping with Brent's ability at the time."

Steve Mammen, Scott Blunk, Kevin Bein, Paul Muehl, Chris Jones, Rich Littlestone, and most likely a good number of other climbers have over the years done a close version of the route with a top-rope. Most have agreed that the climbing is difficult whatever the exact combination of holds used and even with the immense psychological help of a belay from above. In the process of these ascents, it is believed by several climbers, a few holds (or pebbles) have broken off. Yet Pete DeLannoy believes that most if not all of the broken holds have occurred on the lower half of the route rather than on the more difficult upper half.

As to Gill's exact line of ascent, several climbers had gone on the word of the late Kevin Bein who some years prior to his death claimed to have spoken with Gill. Kevin was told, according to Needles local climber John Page, that the route moved left (into the groove of the left-hand route) after reaching the point where the climber is standing on the "hold of commitment" halfway up the wall. Gill is certain that he did not say this, or do this, but he did tell Kevin that he may have used a hold on the right outside corner of the groove as a left handhold. Pete DeLannoy recalls Kevin saying that Gill called anything with the left hand "game."

After Sherman made an ascent of the line thought to be proper by Page, Sherman phoned Gill and was told by Gill that an effort was made to stay out of the left hand groove the whole way. The ridgeline was gained at a point above where the groove topped out. The two routes then merged, according to Gill, for a brief scramble to the summit. After talking to Gill, Sherman told John Page what he had learned. Oddly, as Sherman discovered, Page had difficulty believing that the line stayed out of the groove. But Sherman returned to the route and climbed it as closely to Gill's directions as possible.

Gill stated in a letter to me (Ament) in February 1992:

"Although I do not recall the exact placement of holds on the upper part, the entire purpose of my climb—a private challenge—was to avoid as much as possible the other easier climb, without putting myself in extreme jeopardy. That I planned a pure line in the middle of the face is erroneous. I felt that was too dangerous. The way I went, I could have moved at one point into the easy groove—an escape exit (shades of option soloing?). This just tipped the psychological balance enough for me to commit to a distinct set of moves to the shoulder above. I do recall there was some crystal I pinched out on the face with my right hand. Perhaps it's gone now. Who knows?"

Sherman admitted that the deadly guard railing had been removed (and was gone prior to all of the several "repeat" ascents). He had the benefit of knowing that the route could be climbed. He wore climbing shoes vastly superior to those used in 1961 by Gill. And the large number of competitive boulderers of the modern age certainly sharpened the general consciousness and intensity of a given boulderer's efforts. Sherman had, in addition, the very slight psychological edge of a 2-foot-by-3-foot, padded carpet-patch he placed at the bottom of the rock. Sherman's own strict integrity was to question whether he stayed on the final terrifying move or moves at the top. He may himself have joined the left-hand, easier route a hold or two early. He stated in a letter to Gill, "I joined that route at the shoulder where it becomes trivial."

John Sherman On The Thimble, 1991

Perhaps it should be viewed as a small tribute to Gill that a little mystery about the Thimble remains. In his usual faith-instilling manner, Gill was happy to give Sherman full credit for the ascent. Throughout his climbing, Gill never was uncomfortable with the success of other people or reluctant to give credit where credit was due. Here again, it pleased him to share with another climber the exhilaration of having done something remarkable.

Ribs

In February 1992, while walking through the University of Southern Colorado campus, Gill climbed several extremely smooth cement structures—ribs that had challenged him years before when he was in stronger shape. These involved cross-pressure and friction techniques at a true gymnastic level of difficulty. With Dorothy in a mood for taking photographs, John also climbed up to a high horizontal bar and, at age 55, pulled into a perfect front-lever.

The muscles of his body were sore for several days after, but he learned something. The joy of attempting these difficult moves made the forty years that he had been climbing vanish.

"Difficult Rib" on campus

Front Lever

Climbers Of A New Age Honor Gill

A number of articles had appeared about Gill. Jon Krakauer, for example, wrote a piece in *New Age Journal*, March 1985 (it would later appear in 1990 as a chapter in his book *Eiger Dreams).* Krakauer noted, "It's not unusual to hear buzz-cut adolescent rock prodigies quoting Gill verbatim from one of the articles about bouldering he's written for mountaineering journals."

The June 1986 *High Magazine*, published in England, contained an interview of Gill by Jim Perrin in which so many of Gill's thoughts again materialized. An obscure treatise on Gill had appeared November 10, 1985, in the *Los Angeles Herald*. The author of the article, Lori Karney, called Gill "the father of American rock climbing," seeming to obtain some of her information from Yosemite star John Bachar. In the March 1989 *Outside*, Doug Robinson wrote one of the more intelligent pieces on Gill—strangely as part of a study of modern climbing gear. Robinson mused, "Sure, he'll take stickier shoes when they come along, but he knows their advantage only distracts him from the point. He'll still rise or fall—quite literally—on his own ability, effort, and cool.... Gill's example shows how technologically lean climbing can be, even at an advanced level of mastery."

Most of these commentaries were completely admiring of Gill, even though a great deal of hatred and petty resentment had come to infuse the climbing world. Climbing now was a very different place than ever before. Hoards of extremely dedicated and talented climbers were populating the scene worldwide, many of these individuals, but certainly not all, crass and ready to criticize or sandbag. There too often was a desire to demean the achievements of friends or of past climbers, or to belittle anyone who was not able to boulder or climb at the highest levels—a spirit contrary to everything that Gill and others of us stood for. The spirit of camaraderie among a few souls in relative solitude was replaced by a mass of sometimes-ruthless individuals scrambling and backstabbing for the top. It was difficult for a few 1960's boulderers even to visit their old areas, where now so many climbers came and revealed so little respect for what "things was like back when...." To be forced to spend five minutes with a good many of these "elite" individuals would be about four minutes and fifty-five seconds longer than necessary. Yet Gill greeted many of these new stars as a friend, and in some cases this proved a strength to them and helped them to grow.

Whereas Gill and I (Ament) once had (in the late '60s) declined to participate in Harvey Carter's first ever "bouldering competition," such activities now were commonplace. For example, a bouldering competition was organized at Fort Collins (in its second year, 1992, sponsored by Anhueser Busch). The beer executives were unimpressed with the sportsmanship of the climbers, and the "Horsetooth Hang," as it was called, was canceled. Two years later, it was revived, as the Horsetooth Hang Bouldering Festival, but with the goal being "fun" and no money awarded. Climbers took on a less vicious demeanor, since there was nothing to gain, and the festival became a day of camaraderie and friendly competition.

In 1995, Gill was invited to be guest of honor at this Horsetooth Hang Festival. With his usual graciousness he participated quietly around the periphery, meeting with climbers and observing their efforts. Describing this event, in an article in *Climbing Magazine*, Craig Luebben tells a story that is worth relating. One brash lad, tying in at the bottom of the Mental Block, said, "I can't see using a rope on a classic Gill problem." He was unaware that Gill was standing behind him. John laughed, "I used a top-rope on the first ascent."

Luebben relates how he and Gill escaped the festivities and bouldered together in a quieter part of the area. Luebben notes in his article, "Let there be no doubt: the man [Gill] can still crank." They bouldered together also at the 1997 Horsetooth Hang. Both times, John succeeded at the *True*

Torture Chamber exercise, a very difficult traverse, via his own sequence that he had put up years before and that few people are aware of even today. John describes this route as,

"...a contrived, gymnastic traverse ending with an ascent of a short overhang, at the road-cut at Horsetooth. A difficulty rating, I suspect, of about 5.13. The entire exercise represented technical levels in the late 1960's. What most climbers call the 'Torture Chamber' today is longer but not nearly as demanding as this shorter contrivance."

Gill on the *True Torture Chamber*, Fort Collins, 1995, age 58

True Torture Chamber, age 58

America's great female climber, Lynn Hill, a woman virtually as modest and gracious as Gill, did a nice article on John in a 1995 issue of the French *Roc 'n Wall.* In the interview portion of this article, Gill mentions that he recovered from his torn biceps muscle enough to do "a slightly degraded one-arm pull-up" again. He added,

"Nowadays I particularly like 'option soloing' on the rock with a variety of potential paths, especially when it involves exploration of new territory. However, I still go out to the boulders occasionally—usually to my regret afterwards!"

Other interviews were appearing, such as in Eric Horst's small book *Flash Training.* Here Horst refers to Gill as "the Father of Training for Climbing."

Rock & Ice Magazine in 1997 used a photo of Gill in their continuing article on the history of American climbing, although failing to realize the true Gill contributions—such as the first 5.12 routes....

Austrian Heinz Zak wrote an attractive, coffee-table hardcover book entitled *Rock Stars--the World's Best Free Climbers,* first published in German. He then sent Gill an English language version. Seventy-eight climbers from around the globe were profiled, beginning with Gill. Zak had visited Pueblo and taken several good photos of John on *Captain Winter's Route* (among the Quiet Towers, west of Pueblo).

John Sherman wrote (in 1994) about Gill in his *Stone Crusade*, an excellent, book-length "historical guide to bouldering in America," published by the American Alpine Club. Gill wrote the foreword for this book, stating,

"Most new climbers discover the path where the lights are brightest: among the fashionable inclinations of the experienced many, joining a small army of jargon-spouting enthusiasts who march toward common goals,

in perfect step with the media beat. But a few make a subtle turn and steal away on sojourns of a more eccentric character."

In 1997, Sherman again wrote about Gill, including a photo of John on a Hagermeister boulder, for his (Sherman's) Chockstone book *Better Bouldering*. Sherman calls Gill's boulder routes "the most sought-after testpieces in American bouldering."

Spiritual Apotheosis, A Reflection

John Gill muses,

"Each summer I spend time scrambling and climbing by myself on isolated granite outcrops in the high prairie some distance from my home. Massive domes arch nearly eight hundred feet into the cerulean sky, their smooth flanks golden in the sunlight. I hike and ascend in a profound silence, broken only by the occasional sound of wind among trees and cliffs. There are virtually no humans, no dogs, and only a few cattle here and there in these vast, arid reaches. I think I am climbing on some far off planet, light-centuries from sentient beings. At times, I still my mind. I banish reason and the visual details of my normal life, and my 'I' folds quietly into the stone in a momentary reverie.

"I one day put up a variation on one of the Quiet Towers (Captain Winter's Tower), moving out on an extremely exposed, vertical face (to avoid the tunnel of the normal route). A slight shelf would take me to a small, easy overhang. Several feet out from the beginning of the traverse, both footholds came off simultaneously. Fortunately I move very conservatively on exploratory solo climbs, and I had good handholds. So there was only a

moment of psychic discomfort. I do this easy but exposed pitch regularly now with no qualms.

"Each visit, I climb the steep southern flank of the most spectacular dome. I choose a path that I climbed as an exploratory gesture several seasons past. I carry no rappel rope or other gear—the smooth, steep rock, sprinkled with edges where it forms faint, rounded ridgelines, is hostile to such paraphernalia. Sticky-soled shoes and balance are what counts. A calm upward vision and continuous movement win the prize here—marvelous views from the top, amid graceful, swirling hollows carved into the living granite over eons. In the early summer, large pools of clear water rest here. Sometimes I boulder a little as I move down an easy side of the mountain—not as gutsy as I was thirty years ago—but enough to barely awaken the sleeping tiger.

"In the midst of this solitary grandeur, I visit an even more secluded garden of stone with bouldering potential halfway along a lengthy ridge connecting two domes. As I climb to the top of an easy, twenty-foot vertical cliff, I seize a huge block embedded at the rim and begin to pull up. There is a sickening give to my handhold and a ton of granite slides three inches forward, with a sound exactly like the movement of a stone sepulcher in a nineteen-forties horror movie. In fact, this is precisely what I think at this instant....

"Several years ago, I hiked the long slope leading up to the short north face of the tallest peak in the range. I carried a light rappel line, a sling or two, a sandwich, and water—the last being an absolute essential in this high expanse, a virtual desert. I don't mind the absence of water. The aridity and four-wheel drive roads keep the region uninhabited and tourist-free. At the base of the brief upper wall, I put on my shoes and sprinted up a very modest route to the top—where a ridge-scramble put me on the summit. As I ate my sandwich in the brilliant calm

of the early afternoon, I looked down a long slope leading to a small shadowy canyon where a dirt track ended at an ancient log cabin.

"Something moving caught my eye, and as I looked a bit closer, I saw what appeared to be a camouflage net strung between several trees. A gentle breeze rippled its surface every few seconds. I thought that the canyon might lie outside BLM jurisdiction, and that a rancher had put up an army surplus awning to shade a few cattle from the intense mid-day sun. I was momentarily tempted to rappel down the upper slopes and hike into the canyon for a closer look, but that would have put me at a considerable distance from my parked Explorer. So I ignored the anomaly and returned the way I had come.

"Two years later, I was strolling slowly down the main dirt road leading into the area. A rancher drove up in a pickup, stopped, and struck up a conversation. He told me of the agate hunters who have systematically cleaned the surface of the prairie. He spoke of a rare variety of the stone that is found only here and at some location in China.

"Then, after a brief pause, he told of another rancher who had flown over the mountains a couple years ago and noticed a camouflage net strung where there shouldn't have been one. He notified the county sheriff, who then dispatched two deputies—one being the cousin of the teller of this tale. They found a large arms and ammunition dump concealed under the net, and no sign of the men who had created the stash. A few days later, a ten-vehicle law enforcement caravan made its way over the rough desert track to the dump. FBI and ATF agents, state patrol officers, county deputies, and other officials participated in an investigation of the area that yielded little information. It took several vans to remove the illegal weapons. The raid was apparently suppressed in the

media, but for a very short article in the newspaper of a city sixty miles away. Only a few rifles and shotguns were mentioned....

"Three years ago, I climbed a line parallel to a bolted route on a ridge of the most impressive dome. It was late afternoon, and I had ascended the north face that morning. After descending, I had eaten lunch in the dry, meadow-like shelf at the base of the face's three hundred-foot upper wall. The early afternoon had been spent searching for Indian artifacts and exploring rock formations on the shelf. It was now the time of day that has always revealed the most magic for me over my forty-two year sojourn as a climber. The sky was an utterly clear, deep blue. The wind had died, and the stone was burnished gold and warm to the touch. I was in complete isolation, enveloped in silence, and was intensely aware of the merging of consciousness and environment. I laced my shoes, dusted chalk on my fingers, and started up the smooth rock.

"No equipment today—I am a minimalist at heart. The surface of the mountain gradually steepened, and my progress slowed as I focused on small irregularities and edges. The rock swept up momentarily to a high angle, and I made a balanced move. Reaching for a ledge, I took an involuntary, sharp breath at that precarious instant. The word 'breathless' reverberated through my mind.

"Above, there was accommodating friction and an optional diversion on a short, overhanging step. On top for the second time that day, I was connected to my childhood and to those hours I had wiled away scrambling over the facades and walls of the University of Texas on quiet summer Sunday afternoons in 1949. The same spirit of play, an abandonment of responsibility, and a surge of irrational romanticism... the imagination become reality.

"I have always danced to a tune that few other

climbers seem to hear. By the late 1960's, I had completely abandoned traditional roped climbing in favor of my ongoing bouldering quest and a mature commitment to solitary climbing on larger formations. My first real solo had been a probing excursion up the East Face of Longs Peak in 1954. By 1960, I had become preoccupied with what seemed to me to be the most riveting and demanding pursuit toward which our sport might ultimately evolve—exploratory free soloing at high levels of difficulty. My short climb on the Thimble was the apogee of these efforts, and afterwards I had prepared myself for the luxury of diminished expectations. As a relatively sane free-soloist, I have since willingly traded difficulty for continuity of movement and spiritual apotheosis.

"In the 1970's, I opened new doors of perception through meditative exercises and the astounding experience Carlos Castenada calls the art of dreaming. Although these procedures led at first to inner revelations (alternate realities of exquisite character), eventually my external climbing life was affected as well. I would speak of these things with younger climbers occasionally and would be asked the inevitable question: 'Did this help you climb better?' The answer is no. It doesn't really enhance your technique or increase your courage. It is of far greater value than that. It makes the act of climbing such a marvelous experience that the most pedestrian ascent is enchanting. Solitude intensifies the effect."

Perhaps the definitive turning point in Gill's climbing occurred not simply from seeing gymnastics in 1954 and speculating about how such techniques and strengths could be useful in climbing. It was, at some deeper inner level, to change his perception of climbing from "an extension of walking" (a phrase coined in the film *Dream Of White Horses*, by the brilliant climber Henry Barber) to an extension of gymnastics. Gill very probably was the first person in this country to make such a philosophical transition (during the period 1954-1958). Gill concludes wryly,

"After I pretty much gave up bouldering, ten years ago, I found myself slipping back to Barber's perspective—that climbing is an extension of walking—and am quite comfortable with that."

Duffers

Gill turned sixty on February 16, 1997, and was still climbing well. He had more time now to climb, since he was semi-retired—working one semester a year at USC. He was continuing to do research but confided in me that teaching so much had begun to get him down—for reasons he did not elaborate upon. Yet he would be honored by a November 1997 cover story, *John Gill—Mathematical Climber*, in *Math Horizons*, a publication of the Math Association of America.

I informed John of my desire to bring forth the Third Edition of *Master of Rock*, and we speculated as to what information we might add. He wrote to me,

"You could accompany me out to the Quiet Towers and take a few photos of the old man soloing, if you think it wouldn't gross out young climbers! This might give a visual commentary to climbing as a life-long avocation, and not simply a passion of youth."

In late October, 1997, John and I made plans to meet in Pueblo. "Bring your climbing shoes," he said, "there are some places we can stop and boulder—real easy stuff for old duffers." My pride was shattered for an instant, except that I knew Gill had hit the mark. I had spent the last couple years writing, getting settled into a new marriage, buying a house, bringing a daughter into the world, eating, gaining weight, learning how to use a fancy new computer, things like that, and very little climbing. As we drove toward the parking spot below the towers, we spoke of a few health problems I'd been suffering from—high blood pressure was one. Gill told me I was going to have to discipline myself and get back into shape.

He spoke about soloing some of the routes on the Quiet Towers. He estimated that he had climbed one of these towers, a six hundred-foot route, more than a hundred and fifty times over the last twenty-five years.

The approach up a hill to the rocks was steep. I was breathing hard, moving slow, my heart pounding. Somehow I reached the summit of a rock high above the floor of the canyon, across from the tower John was to solo. He moved deliberately, quite relaxed, up a steep, three hundred and fifty-foot wall of granite. I used a telephoto lens to take pictures.

Gill reaches the summit of one of his Quiet Towers

In earlier years, some people who were looking for an excuse to dismiss John's bouldering speculated that he suffered from acrophobia. It was never true. Solo climbs in the Tetons through the years, the Thimble, and in later years many ascents without a rope up walls of granite showed that he truly was a full-fledged rock climber and never "only a boulderer."

John spoke about his dog Collette. He had left her home this day. She often accompanied him up to the Quiet Towers and found her way to places she knew John would reach or where she could see him as he climbed. She sometimes managed to get to a summit by way of the backside.

Soon after my visit to Pueblo, John sent me an e-mail. In it he wrote,

"I am concerned about your physical condition, Pat. Please promise me you will start an exercise regimen. None of us is what he was, but I remember the splendid athlete and climber of past years and know you have it in you to recapture some of that inner glory. Middle age can be a wonderful time of renaissance. I found it in my early and mid-fifties, and so has Tom Frost, from what I hear. Your excellent new book (on mastery in climbing) says it all—you are a great master, and you must not abandon your physical craft, for the sake of us all. You have such a wonderful appreciation of the subtle aspects of climbing; you must hone these to fit your age and responsibilities (although I admit it is not easy to do this in an area where there is much frenetic climbing activity). I hope you can come back down and scramble around the base of these cliffs with me. There are some lengthy, pleasant low traverses plus a few challenging spots. We might even see a bighorn or a sluggish bear."

In just a few sentences, I was reminded once again what kind of person John Gill is. A friend. An inspiration!

Index

A

Acrobat Overhang, 74, 113
Air Force R.O.T.C., 21
Alman, Annie Berryhill, 5-7
Alman, William Jefferson, 5-7
Ament, Pat, i, iv, x-xiii, 73-74, 106-110, 113, 123-127, 132-133, 138-141, 147-150, 153, 166-167, 184, 191, 193, 198, 207-209
American Alpine Club, 8, 167, 201
American Alpine Journal, 28, 118, 119
Angel Overhang, 62
Anhueser Busch, 198
Appalachians, 8
ATF, 204
Atlanta Constitution, 8
Austin, 4
Azaryin, Albert, 21

B

Bachar, John, 152, 197
Banks, Warren, x, 130, 150
Barber, Henry, 206-207
Bates, Barry, 124
Battleship, 135
Baxter, 27, 39
Baxter's Pinnacle, North Face, 39
Bay Area, 188
Bayonet, the, 64
Beehive Cliffs, the, 8
Bein, Kevin, 122, 191, 192
Bell Smith Springs, 80, 89
Belmont area, Pueblo, 134
Bend, Oregon, 21
Better Bouldering, 202
Billings, Montana, 185
Birmingham, 66
Black Streak, 155
Blacktail Butte, 31-32, 43, 178
BLM, 204
Blunk, Scott, x, 162, 192
Boggs, Chris, 188
Boggs, Dorothy (also Dorothy Gill), vii, x, 134, 140-141, 153, 165, 166, 179, 184-185, 188, 195
Boggs, Dylan Munroe, 188-190
Boggs, Marci, 188
Boggs, Nicole Rose, 188
Boggs, Susanne, 134, 188
Bonatti, Walter, 121
Borghoff, Mike, 40
Borgman, Rich, x, 95, 106-107, 124, 126-127, 129, 132
Boulder Canyon (see Castle Rock)
Boulder, Colorado, xi, 73, 121 (see Third Flatiron, Castle Rock, Flagstaff Mountain, Eldorado Canyon)
Bradley, Bob, 54
Brat, 73
Bread Loaf, 60
Breashears, David, x, xii, 147
Bridwell, Jim, 124
Briggs, Bill, 187
British Mountaineering Council, 166
Broadway, 13-14
Brooklyn Center for the Performing Arts, 188
Buckingham, Bill, 187
Budapest, 185
Buhl, Hermann, 33, 121
Bulge, 81
Bulletin of the Calcutta Math Society, 186
Buxton, England, 166

C

Cables Route, 14-15
Calanques, 172
Camp 4, 123-124
Candelaria, Bob, x, 140
Captain Winter's Route, 201
Captain Winter's Tower, 202
Carter, Harvey, 198

Casteneda, Carlos, 164
Castle Rock, 73-75 113 (see also *Final Exam* and *Acrobat Overhang*)
Cave-In Rock State Park, 80
Center Route, Red Cross Rock, 38, 69, 123, 162, 167-168
Chardin, Tielhard de, 185
Charlet-Moser piton, 174
Cheney, Steve, 130
Chessler, Michael, 153
Chicago, 33, 90
Chouinard, Yvon, x, 27-29, 31, 42, 145
City of Rocks, 94
Cleveland, Pete, 92-93, 179
Climbing Art Magazine, the, 162, 171, 183
Climbing Magazine, 154, 191-198
Cloudland Canyon, 10, 16-17
Cloudveil Dome, 22
Collette, 189, 209
Colorado, iv, vi, xi, 1, 12, 20, 54-66, 73, 91, 96-209 (see Split Rocks, Estes Park, Fort Collins, Pueblo, Boulder, Flagstaff Mountain, Eldorado Canyon,Hager-meister boulders, the Needle…)
Colorado Springs, 130, 134, 178, 184
Colorado State University, 95, 107, 130
Communications in …Continued Fractions, 186
Cooper, Gary, 26
Custer, Wyoming, 179
Cutfinger Rock, 30

D

D'Antonio, Bob, 150
Delannoy, Pete, x, 191-192
Delicate Arete, vii, 27, 171
Delicate Wall, 63, 108-110
Deliverance, 16
Deming, Dr. Edward, 185
Desoto Canyon, 66
Diamond, 13
Direct North Overhang, Scab, 49
Direct Route, Devil's Lake, 36
Disappointment Peak, 28
Dixon Dam, 103, 117
Dixon Springs, 80-83, 86-88, 90
Dusty, 169

E

Edlinger, Patrick, 167
Eiger Dreams, 197
Eldorado Canyon, 125
Elephant Rocks, 80
Eliminator, Left, 100-101, 106, 122
Eliminator, Right, 103, 106, 129
Ellery Queen, 5
Emerson, Dick, 22
England, vii, 165-166, 197
Erickson, Jim, x, 69
Estes Park, vi, 12, 20, 54, 56, 59, 60, 62-63, 66, 70, 91, 109, 120, 126, 143, 147, 179
Everest, 121

F

Falcon, 78
Falling Ant Slab (see *No-Hands Variation)*, 29, 31
Fatted Calf, the, 130, 138-139, 153, 156-157, 182-183
FBI, 204
Fenton, Renn, 65
Final Exam, 74-75
Flagstaff Amphitheater, 124
Flagstaff Mountain, xi, 106, 124, 130, 137
Flash Training, 201
Flatiron, 36, 69
Flying Buttress, 44, 92
Flying Buttress Variation, 92

Fort Collins, x, xii, 95, 98, 103, 106-107, 117-122, 126, 129-130, 152, 167-168, 183, 198-199 (see also Horsetooth Reservoir, *Eliminator,* Mental Block….)
Fort Mountain, 8, 11
Fort Peck Dam, 42
Frisch, Lora Sara, x, 66, 79, 130, 133-134
Frossen, Bob, 14

G

Galena Park, 4
Gallo, 140
Garden of the Gods, 179
Garnet Canyon, 27, 40
Garnet Canyon, north wall, 40
Gem Lake Boulders, xiii, 59-60, 120
Gem Lake Trail, 59-60, 120
Georgia, xi, 8-9, 12, 16, 18-21, 26
Georgia Tech, xi, 16, 18-21
Gill, Bernice Alman, 3-4, 8, 20, 66, 188
Gill Boulder, *Center Direct West Face,* 125
Gill Boulder, *Far Right Side*, 125
Gill Crack, 33
Gill Crack, the, 74
Gill, John Paul (inclusive)
Gill, John Paul Sr., 3-4, 8, 20, 66, 153
Gill, Pam, 60, 79, 106, 118, 130, 133-134, 184, 188
Gill Swing, the, 125
Gill Variation, 73
Glasgow Air Force Base, 38, 45
Gnomon, 44
Godfrey, Bob, iv, viii, x
Goldstone, Rich, 69, 90, 92
Grand Teton National Park, 38 (see also Tetons)
Gray Rock Mountain, 120
Guiseley Indoor Wall, England, 166
Gulfport, Mississippi, 5-7

H

Hagermeisters, 54-58, 143, 147
Hand Traverse, 110
Hangover Pinnacle, 22
Hazel, Al, 14
Hermann, Buhl, 33, 121
Hidden Overhang, 86
Higgins, Tom, x, 113, 124
High Magazine, 167, 197
Hill, Lynn, 201
Hoffman, Lew, x, 150, 178
Holloway, Jim, x, 150, 182
Holubar, 19
Hooper, 79
Horsetooth Reservoir, 95, 106, 117-118, 127, 132 (see Fort Collins, *Eliminator*, Mental Block, etc.)
Horst, Eric, 201
Horthy, Admiral, 185
Houston, Texas, 4
Hungary, 185

I

Incisor, the, 44
Inner Game of Tennis, the, 145
Inner Outlet Boulder, 78
International Center for Math. Research, 172

J

Jackson Hole, 25-26, 178
Jenny Lake, 22, 24, 29, 42-43, 64, 178
Jenny Lake boulders, 22, 29, 64
Jensen Ridge, 24
Jewel T., 25
Jones, Alicia, 181
Jones, Chris, x, 150, 168, 179-183, 192
Journal of Applied Numerical Math, 186
Juan, Don, 164
Juggernaut, 148, 152
Jumbo, 83

K

Kamps, Bob, x, 28, 43, 65
Karney, Lori, 197
Kentucky, 79, 80, 84-85,
Kertzman, Brent, 191-192
Keyhole, 72
Khayyam Spire, 44
Kingpin, the, 44
Kipling, Rudyard, 5
Kirk, Captain, 113
Kline, Kris, 191
K-Mart, 150, 171
Knob, the, 29
Krakauer, Jon, ix, 197

L

Lake Marie, 136
Lanoue, Fred, 18
Left Eliminator, 100-101
Left Side, Fatted Calf Boulder, 105-106, 156
Little Flatiron, 33
Little Overhang, 130, 138, 155
Little Owl Canyon, 159-160, 190
Little Rockies, 40
Long, John, 152, 154
Longs Peak, 12-15, 206
Longs Peak, East Face, 12-15, 206
Los Angeles Herald, 197
Lost Canyon, vii, 148-149, 152
Lowe, Greg, 124
Luminy Campus, France, 173

M

Maiden, the, 12
Mammen, Steve, 192
Maroon Bells, 14
Master of Rock, viii, ix, 207
Math Horizons, 207
Mathematica Scandinavia, 186
Math. Association of America, 186
Maugham, Somerset, 167
Mayrose, Paul, x, 54
McGreggor Rock, 20, 66
Meeker Park, 12
Mental Block, 104-106, 129, 168, 183, 198
Mental Block, *Center Route*, vi, 38, 104-105
Mental Block, *Left Side*, 105-106, 156
Mental Block, *Pinch Overhang*, 104, 106, 183
Milk River, 42
Milton Boulder, 125
Mirror Face, 113
Mirror Lake, 14
Mississippi, 5-7
Molar, 53
Montana, 38-41, 121, 144, 185
Mount Thielson, south face, 21
Muehl, Paul, x, 192
Murray, Bob, 150
Murray, Kentucky, 79, 90

N

Needle, the Estes Park, 91
Needles, the, vi, 20, 33, 44-53, 64-65, 73, 76-78, 92-93, 106, 140, 162, 168, 191-195
Neureichenau, 185
New York, 70-71, 121-122, 133, 188
North Face, Baxter's Pinnacle, 39
North Georgia, 10-11
North Wall, Garnet Canyon , 40

O

Ohio, 80, 90
Ohio River, 80
Oregon, 21
Ortenberger, Leigh, 187
Outlet Boulder, 51, 92
Outstanding Faculty Award, 187

P

Page, John, 192-193
Parkview Episcopal Hospital, 184-185
Paydirt Pinnacle, 50-51
Pebble Wall, 124
Pennirile Forest State Park, 80, 84-85
Pennsylvania, 3
Penny Ante Boulder, 163
Perrin, Jim, 167, 197
Perry, Don, 21
Persian Wall, 87-88
Piana, Paul, x, 65
Pike, Keith, 191
Pownall, Richard, 22
Pratt, Chuck, 124
Princeton Mountaineering Club, 20
Proceedings, Norwegian Royal Society, Arts, Letters, 186
Pueblo, iv, vii, ix, 130-165
Pueblo West, vii, 165-209

Q

Queenpin, 76
Quiet Towers, the, vii, 149, 201-209

R

Rachael, 53
RDs, vi, 92, 93
Reach Overhang, 96, 117
Rearick's Challenge, 69
Rearick, Dave, vi, x, 42, 54, 57, 69-70, 129, 187
Rebuttal, 80, 82
Red Cross Rock, vi, vii, 29, 38, 69, 123, 162, 167-168 (see *Center)*
Red, Overhanging Wall, 127
Regis College, 184
Reynolds, Burt, 79
Right Eliminator, 103, 106, 129
Ripper Traverse, 130-132, 138, 140, 151, 158, 190
Robbins, Royal, 1, 39, 65, 73, 76, 106, 108, 121
Robinson, Doug, 197
Rock & Ice Magazine, 201
Rock 'n Wall, 201
Rock Springs, 26
Rock Stars--the World's Best Free Climbers, 201
Rocky & Bullwinkle, 66
Rocky Mtn. Journal of Math, 186
Rocky Mtn. National Park, 12, 20
Rohrl, Helmut, 33, 187

S

Satisfaction Buttress, 28, 173
Scab, *Direct North Overhang*, 49
Shades Mountain, 66-68
Shannon, Curt, x, 150-151, 182, 189
Shawangunks, 70-73, 121-122
Shearer, Jeannie, 8
Sherman, John, x, 191-195, 201-202
Shragg, Ray, 64, 90
Sierra Nevada, the, 123
Sigma Xi Chapter, 186
Silent Climber, the, 153
Smith Overhang, 124-125, 128
Smith, Thorne, 5
Snowy Range, Wyoming, 120, 136
Sometime Crack, 33, 36, 69
South Dakota (see Needles)
Southern Illinois, 80, 89 (see Dixon Springs, Bell Smith Springs)
Southwest Face Direct, Paydirt Pinn., 50
Spike, the, 53
Spire Four, One, Two, 44
Split Rocks, 1, 63, 107-112, 126
Stannard, John, 187
Star Trek, 113
Stone Crusade, 201
Stone Mountain, xi, 19-20
Storage Shed Variation, 51
Storm Point, 40, 175
Stretcher, 179
Stumbling Block, 53
Sundance Buttress, 179

Sunshine Boulder, 98
Supremacy Crack, xi
Sylvan Lake Boulder, 48, 52
Symmetry Spire, 24

T

Tea Kettle, 115
Teewinot, east face, 20
Teewinot, north face, 22
Ten Pins, 92
Tetons, vi, xi, 2, 20-30, 38-42, 48, 64, 66-69, 123, 162, 167-168, 171, 173, 178, 209
Thimble, the, 1, 33, 44-47, 65, 73, 106, 123, 162, 191-195, 206, 209
Third Flatiron, 12
Toepel, Bob, 24
Tombstone, 33, 36
Torture Chamber, 199 (see *True)*
Transactions, 186
Triconi Nail, 77
Trinidad, Colorado, 133
Trinity Buttress, 173, 176
True Torture Chamber exercise, 106, 199-200
Tuscaloosa, 3-4, 66, 79, 153
Twin Sisters, 179

U

U.S. Rangers, 40
University of Alabama, 3, 65-66
University of Chicago, 27, 33, 38
University of Chicago Gymnastics Team, 33
University of Geneva, 153
University of Georgia, 8, 21, 27
University of Marseilles, 173
University of Southern Colorado, 130, 148, 186, 195
University of Texas, 4, 205
Unsoeld, Willi, 22

V

Veedauwoo, Wyoming, vii, 113-116, 132
Vulgarians, 42

W

Walling, Ritner, 28
Warrior Run, 3
Wayne, John, 26
Weeks, Ken, 42
Wenzel umbrella tent, 66
Williams, Bob, x, 128-129, 132, 150-152
Williams, R.F., 90-91, 187
Wimer, Dick, 12, 14
Wind River range, 133
Window Route, the, 13
Wisconsin, 20, 33, 34, 69, 121
Woodruff, Bill, 42
World War II, 185
Wright, Fred, 33
Wunsch, Steve, x, 122
Wyoming, 20, 48, 113, 120-121, 133, 136, 171

Y

Yellow Wall, the, 48, 52

Z

Zak, Heinz, 201
Zillertal, 24
Zion National Park, 65
Zortman, Montana, 40, 41
Zschiesche, Eric, 191